Function Analysis System Technique

For Breakthrough Solutions

FUNCTION ANALYSIS SYSTEM TECHNIQUE

For Breakthrough Solutions

Anil Kumar Mukhopadhyaya
CMA, CVS-Life; FINVEST

I.K. International Publishing House Pvt. Ltd.
NEW DELHI

Published by
I.K. International Publishing House Pvt. Ltd.
S-25, Green Park Extension
Uphaar Cinema Market
New Delhi 110 016 (India)
E-mail: info@ikinternational.com
Website: www.ikbooks.com

ISBN 978-93-86768-01-8

Published by Krishan Makhijani for I.K. International Publishing House Pvt. Ltd. S-25, Green Park Extension, Uphaar Cinema Market, New Delhi 110 016. Printed by Rekha Printers Pvt. Ltd., Okhla Industrial Area, Phase II, New Delhi 110 020.

Dedicated to

My Wife

Santa Mukhopadhyaya

She is the driving force to complete this book.

Foreword

Since long, a lot of thrust is being given by the industries, organisations and societies to lead the future by 'innovation'.

In the present scenario, 'innovation' is not a choice or option but has become mandatory for survival and growth. Therefore, to build 'innovation' in a product, process or system the approach finally boils down to the very fundamental for the existence of everything, i.e., 'functions'. Identifying and classifying the 'functions' and building them for enhancing performance like convenience, reliability, serviceability, etc., are key to evolving 'breakthrough' solutions to problems. To build desired technical functions for achieving customer functions that may be current or futuristic, Customer Function Analysis System Technique (FAST) diagrams & Technical FAST diagrams were created. Finally, effective application of the same is used to obtain 'breakthrough' solution.

Breakthrough solution is often tempted to be achieved through product benchmarking; which appears to be a shortcut and clearly fails in most of the cases in achieving the desired objective. 'Function analysis' based approach from output of FAST diagrams has now become an essential attribute to success.

In the present book, the author has put in his best efforts to explain how to build the desired technical functions and use these to explore breakthrough solutions through real-life examples, in simple language; elaborating relationship between function and breakthrough solutions in a lucid manner.

Surely, the book will serve as a useful reference and guide to the value practitioners in industries not only for understanding the methodology but also for applying the same to obtain breakthrough or innovative solutions as required for sustainability with competitive advantage.

S C Sarkar
Past President
Indian Value Engineering Society

Preface

I have observed during my lectures that value engineers in various workshops and seminars are not yet mature enough to derive maximum benefit from the use of FAST. It reminds me the saying of Charles W. Bytheway that he uses FAST for breakthrough solutions.

Value and mismatches is comparatively a new concept which clarifies what exactly "value" is meant for. An introduction of these topics is made in the first chapter. It is expected that some new thoughts will emerge for the benefit for value improvement.

FAST is a function block diagram. The nucleus of the diagram is the "function". The correct identification is the prime objective of getting maximum benefit from the FAST. If the function is not correctly defined the result will not come as expected from FAST. In this regard, I have seen that there is still gap in proper function definition. Because of this reason I have given special focus on "function". I also have developed rules for checking whether definition of the function is correct. I have also mentioned how one can improve this ability by taking day-to-day product.

There are three types of FAST: Classical FAST, Technical Oriented FAST, and Customer-Oriented FAST. All the three FASTs have been dealt with in detail using a very common object known to all. It is expected that the readers will have clear vision about this wonderful tool.

Another important thing which I observed is that the readers should be provided with different case studies. The case studies are chosen from different industries. In every case study, the emphasis has been given to define "function". Moreover, it has been clearly explained step by step how to draw FAST diagram.

The readers are interested to have some objective questions to clarify their understanding about the chapter. I have provided various questions after the end of each chapter which will make it reader friendly. The solutions are also given in the last chapter.

I sincerely believe that the readers will get insight of FAST procedure and will be able to come out with breakthrough solutions.

Any suggestions from the readers will be highly appreciated.

Anil Kumar Mukhopadhyaya
E-mail: anilm13@rediffmail.com
Website: www.value-engineering-training.com

Acknowledgements

At the beginning I must acknowledge all my readers who on various occasions mentioned about my all previous books which have helped them to achieve some of their goals. At the same time they requested me to keep on writing some new concepts and difficult and useful topics.

In September 2015, I was nominated as member of VM Standard Committee. The Chairman of the Committee was Mr. Mutiah Kasi. In INVEST Conference in Bangalore in 2015, I had the opportunity to discuss about various FAST Diagram and how to make maximum use of FAST for breakthrough solutions which is the need of the hour. I must acknowledge for his acceptance of some of my thoughts and continuous support to make the subject more meaningful.

I must acknowledge Mr Surya Prabhaker, who understands me and my new thoughts and always tries to implement them at the opportune moments.

I must acknowledge Ms. Anita Lukose who has supported me regarding the matter of this book.

Lastly, I must appreciate my wife Santa to provide support as and when required which has helped me to complete this book.

I request to my readers to provide suggestions for improvement of this book.

Anil Kumar Mukhopadhyaya
E-mail: anilm13@rediffmail.com
Website: www.value-engineering-training.com

Contents

CHAPTER

1

Recapitulation of Value Engineering Concept

"Value analysis is a system for use when better than normal results are needed."
– Lawrence D. Miles

1.1 VALUE

Value is a misnomer. A thing which has some value to some body may have no value to another person. I remember a story which my mother told me when I was a kid. The story goes like this: One day a goldsmith was passing by a village road. It was a muddy road and a number of hens were searching for food. The goldsmith saw that one hen had something, which she tried to break. But when she could not break it, she threw it aside. The goldsmith was amazed to see that it was a glittering object. He got interested and on drawing near saw that it was a small gold ball. He thanked God and mused in his mind that this creature did not know the value of the object. This is what value is. Value to one, is no value to another!

Value also depends on time. A thing which has value today could have no value tomorrow. In the late fifties, I remember the value of a "slide rule." Those were proud students who possessed an "Aristo" slide rule (incidentally, I had one too!). After the invention of the "calculator" everyone knows what happened to the slide rule? It lost its value. It is possible that my great grandson will have its value in 2100, as an antique article.

The refrigerator was a luxury item at some point of time. Over the years because of environmental changes it has become a necessary item today. While it has a good value in most of the parts of India, it does not have the same value in hilly cold areas. It clearly indicates that value changes from place to place too.

The word "value" is not a new one. Aristotle in the year 365 BC advocated seven types of values. In the value engineering concept, only economical value is considered. This economic value is divided into four values which are:

- Use value
- Esteem value
- Exchange value
- Cost value

The value can be defined mathematically as,

$$\text{Value} = \frac{(\text{Performance} + \text{Capability})}{\text{Cost}} = \frac{\text{Function}}{\text{Cost}}$$

In other words value is a ratio. If the ratio is improved, the value will increase. There are five ways to improve this ratio and they are:

1. Function remains same, but cost is reduced.
2. Function improves but cost remains same.
3. Function improves in a greater proportion than the increase of cost.
4. Function reduced, but cost is reduced in a greater proportion.
5. Function improves and cost is reduced.

The fourth one, ratio improvement is not accepted in value engineering. This is because in any way performance reduction is not acceptable. The performance has to remain same or improved.

1.2 COST

If one observes the mathematical model of value, it will be observed that one of the elements is "cost". At the outset, the details of the cost have to be analyzed. The cost of the product can be viewed as below:

Table 1.1: Elements of Cost

Items	Monetary unit
Direct material	
Direct labor	
Direct expenses	
Prime cost	
Production overhead	
Production overhead	
Administrative overhead	
Works cost	
Selling overhead	
Distribution overhead	
Total cost	

The cost elements have been elaborated below, in order to have better understanding.

1.2.1 Direct Materials

What is a direct material? How will one distinguish between a direct material and an indirect material? Is there any indicator? Is direct material always a direct material or an indirect material is always an indirect material?

The material which has a relationship with the number of production is called a direct material. If one kg is required for one component then if it is a direct material then it will take two kg for two components. This is the indicator by which you can differentiate between a direct material and an indirect material.

It is true that a material in one case may become an indirect material in some other instance. If one kg grease is required for one assembly and two kg for two assemblies then it can be considered a direct material. But the same grease used for maintenance purpose of the machine is considered an indirect material.

1.2.2 Direct Labor

The indicator of direct labor is the same as that of direct material. That is labor hours which are required for one component should be doubled if two components are to be manufactured.

1.2.3 Direct Expenses

In cases where expenses can be directly attributed to a particular order for a particular material (or part number or product), the expenses are called direct expenses. For instance, if an order is received for 100 gear shafts and the customer has specified that all the parts need to undergo a series of quality checks. In this case, the expenses for quality checks is directly attributable to the order and the product, and hence categorized under direct expenses.

1.2.4 Production Overhead

Before explaining the production overhead, it is better to understand what is an overhead. In financial parlance the expenses which cannot be directly allocated to any product, process or system is accumulated in the name of an overhead. In other words, you can assume that it is lack of clarity/visibility or ignorance of the finance department. It is just like "factor of safety" in the engineering parlance. The other name of the "factor of safety" is "factor of ignorance". It has become the endeavor of the finance that maximum amount should be directly allocated to the product, process or system. That is why a new attempt has been made in the form of "activity costing", though it has not been universally accepted as a norm.

The overheads include the following items:

- Indirect materials
- Indirect labor
- Indirect expenses

Within the production overhead, all indirect materials, indirect labor and indirect expenses which are directly required for production, are clubbed, for example, the indirect materials like cotton waste, grease, cutting tools, cutting fluid, etc. In indirect expenses labor like men responsible for moving materials from one machine to another, labor responsible for maintaining the machines and equipment, etc., are included. The indirect expenses are like traveling expenses required to be done for production, etc.

1.2.5 Administrative Overhead

As in the production overhead, in the administrative overhead all those indirect materials, indirect labor and indirect expenses which are incurred on the administration of the organization which is responsible for producing the product, process, or system are considered administrative overhead. Here the indirect material is like paper, any other material required to run the office for the administration. The labor portion is all the staff and the officers, as well as the workers of the administrative setup. The indirect expenses are like the traveling expenses required for the executives, etc., other expenses required for the benefit of workers as well as other employees.

1.2.6 Selling and Distribution Overhead

Selling and distribution are essential parts of every business. These expenses are such that it cannot be allocated to any product, process or system. Hence, these expenses are considered the overhead. The break-up of this overhead will also include indirect material, indirect labor and indirect expenses. All the materials used are indirect; similarly, labor is indirect labor and expenses are indirect expenses.

1.3 WORTH

Worth is an essential component of value engineering. It should be properly understood and should be used judiciously. Though it is difficult to attribute a financial figure of worth but it should be done with utmost care. The search for the worth of a product/process/service is the first step to creativity.

Worth may be defined as the minimum cost of achieving a function. The determination of worth depends upon various factors. They may be thought of as below:

- Knowledge factor of the team doing value engineering
- It will be based on geographical position
- It will be based on time factor

The worth of a function can be determined by comparing it with similar items which can do the same function. As an example, the function of a "tie pin" is to "retain the tie". Let us assume the function cost of "retain the tie" is Rs. 10.00 (it may be more, depending upon the tie pin). This function of "retain the tie" can be achieved by a "gems clip" which costs Re. 0.10. Hence, the worth of the function "retain the tie" can be said to be Re. 0.10.

1.4 VALUE MISMATCHES

Value mismatch is comparatively a new concept which clarifies what exactly value is meant for. As it has been mentioned in the value equation is that it has a relation with cost. Table 1.2 indicates what is called value mismatch.

Table 1.2: Value Mismatch

Need/Performance	Cost	Value
High	Low	Value
High	Average	Value/Opportunity to improve
Average	Low	Value/Opportunity to improve
High	High	Opportunity to improve
Average	Average	Opportunity to improve
Low	Low	Opportunity to improve
Low	Average	Opportunity to improve/Mismatch
Average	High	Opportunity to improve/Mismatch
Low	High	Mismatch

The above concept has been shown in Fig. 1.1.

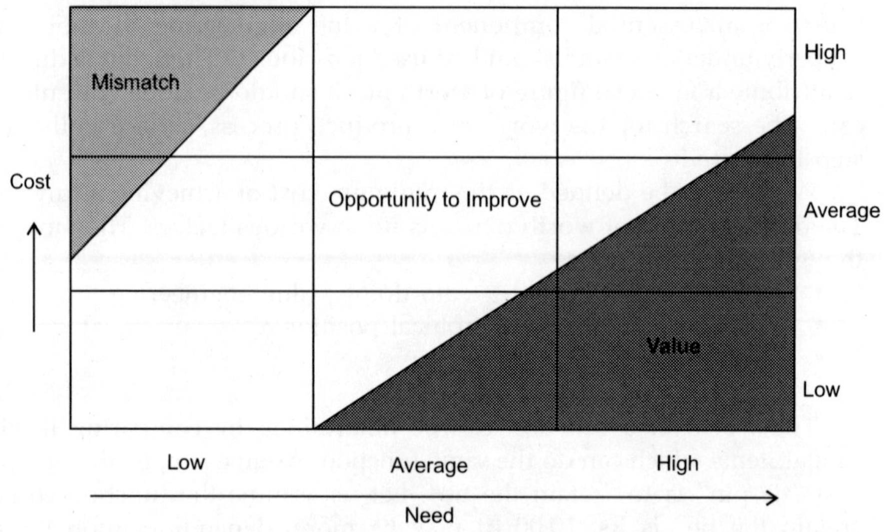

Fig. 1.1. Value Mismatch

During my professional career, I have encountered situations where low need and high cost, was creating a value mismatch because of the desire of the owner. The owner of the project, a layout in steel plant, was based on Vastu Sastra, as per the desire of the owner. That creates an excess cost of ten lakhs in comparison to a layout based on the simple need.

1.5 EXERCISE

1. **Explain with the help of an example the following types of economic value.**
   (a) Use value (b) Cost value
   (c) Exchange value (d) Esteem value
   Is it possible that a product possesses esteem value without use value. Justify your answer with example.

2. **How do you identify the components of value in a software product? Explain the difference in approach compared to a hardware product.**
   (IEB 5 Innovation and Value Engineering, January 2007)

3. **What is an indicator of direct material?**
   (a) Which is included in the product?
   (b) Which is having direct relation with product volume?

(c) Which is purchased for the manufacture of the product?
(d) Which depends upon the choice of the cost accountant?

4. Are indicators of direct material and direct labor are same?
(a) True (b) False

5. What are the constituents of an overhead?
(a) Direct material, direct labor and direct expenses
(b) Indirect material, direct labor and indirect expenses
(c) Indirect material, indirect labor and indirect expenses
(d) Indirect material, indirect labor and direct expenses

6. A material cannot become direct or indirect material because of its use in the product?
(a) True (b) False

7. What is the difference between cost and price?
(a) Cost and price are same.
(b) Price is always less than cost
(c) Price has no relation with cost.
(d) If profit is added with the cost, it becomes price.

8. If the total cost of a product is Rs. 100 and the profit is 15% of total cost, then what is the price of the product?
(a) Rs. 85.00 (b) Rs. 115.00
(c) Rs. 95.00 (d) Rs. 105.00

9. If the total cost of a product is Rs. 100 and the profit is 15% of sales value, then what is the price of the product?
(a) Rs. 115.65 (b) Rs. 116.65
(c) Rs. 117.65 (d) Rs. 118.65

10. Dose worth depend on information?
(a) Yes (b) No

11. Choose the correct statement
(a) Worth is not an indispensable item of the value study.
(b) Direct cost is only required for the value study.
(c) Selection of project takes back seat in the value study.
(d) In the value study, think about functions; not parts.

12. The value of a product can be defined as,
(a) Price by cost (b) Share value of the product
(c) Function by cost (d) Cannot be defined

13. What is direct material cost of the product?
- (a) The cost of materials responsible for producing the product.
- (b) The only basic raw materials cost.
- (c) All the raw materials cost which are responsible for manufacturing the product.
- (d) Those material costs which vary with the number of products produced.

14. Identify the wrong statement.
- (a) Value is a function of time.
- (b) Value is a function of people.
- (c) Value is just subject alone.
- (d) Value is a function of circumstances.

15. Choose the correct statement
- (a) Value engineering is concerned with the only acquisition cost.
- (b) All cost is for function.
- (c) Cost is not an important parameter for value study.
- (d) One should not be bothered about cost.

CHAPTER

2

Function Analysis

2.1 THE BIRTH OF FUNCTION

In order to understand Function, it is necessary to know the history of its evaluation. The following was the discussions between William Sredenscheck of General Electric, USA and Lawrence D. Miles.

Sredenscheck recalled an early conversation with Miles:

"Sreddy, this cost–reduction program has got to be broader than just getting a lower price for purchased material" said Miles.

Sredenscheck reacted, "What are you thinking about? After all, we're purchasing people. It's our job to get the material for lower cost."

Miles said, "But the cost of the material is not the heart of the problem. The real meat of the coconut is to get the lowest cost for providing the *function* that the customer wants in our product." And he hit the word *'function'*.

Again Sredenscheck reacted, "We've got a purchasing job to do. What in the name of sense is this *function* thing you're talking about?"

He said, "Well, it'll take a few minutes. Is now a good time?"

The word **Function** was born. The first impression of some of the experts of Value Analysis/Value Engineering gave more clarity and importance.

The first impression of Ted Fowler is also very interesting. It is:

"Larry spent several days with us, giving various lectures and then leading us in a team effort to do what value analysis does, and that's typically to define functions," he said, recalling that participants were divided into three-man teams tasked with improving the value of various elements of the radar equipment built at the Utica plant.

The word "function" means something very different to a value analyst or a value specialist. It is specifically limited to two words, one a verb and the other a noun, which make up a two-word sentence. And the sentence answers the question, 'What does the product or process do?' If you can define the function in two words, according to Larry, you probably understand it – and if it takes more than two words, you probably don't understand it. That was one of the favorite sayings: he published that in both of his books, and in every lecture he made that point. The definition of the function was the heart of the process, because when you define the function in very elemental form, it allows you to be very, very creative in developing solutions or alternative configurations of the product.

Another expert in this field, Charles W. Bytheway mentioned his first impression about function, which is as below:

"The Value Engineering Job Plan developed by Lawrence D. Miles was taught to us. On about the third day we were taught about functions. It was the first time I had ever heard about expressing things as functions using a verb and a noun. The function concept fascinated me. It was a new way of thinking for me. When I returned from California, I immediately organized a workshop to teach what I had learned."

2.2 INTRODUCTION

Human civilization will forever be indebted to the twentieth century. During this period there was maximum progress of the human race through innovations, creations and discoveries. It is applicable to all fields, that is, technology, sociology, management, and anything that can be thought of.

In the arena of new concepts, one of the most important concepts which emerged in the twentieth century is the Function Analysis—conceived by Lawrence D. Miles. This concept has changed the way of looking at the product, service, and system. Though it started with application on an existing product, service or system, but now it is applicable to all these, right from the conceptual stage.

The heart of value engineering is in its functional approach. This approach differentiates between value engineering and other cost reduction techniques.

2.3 WHAT IS A FUNCTION?

If one looks to the evolution of human race, one will find that there was constant need. When one was fulfilled then came a new one. When they were not protected from the environment they need something which will provide that. They made caves, the purpose was to protect them. The purpose for which something is created is the function. L.D. Miles was the first person who thought of this function to satisfy the need and the desire of the human being.

The creation of any object—be it a hardware or a process or a system is for certain purposes. These purposes may be termed functions. If the functions are achieved as desired by the customer, the item is useful, otherwise it is of no use.

The purpose of a bottle is to hold liquid. If it does not do that, it is useless to the customer, though the customer may have paid adequately and it is appealing to his desires of color and shape.

2.4 HOW TO DEFINE A FUNCTION

Identification of functions of a product, service or system is a vital aspect in value engineering. Correct identification will provide a great help in solving the problem. There are many occasions when the functions that appear to be the functions of the item are not the correct functions.

In order to identify a function, functions are to be defined. If one is asked to define a product, service or system, one can take recourse to a sentence or even a paragraph. But in value engineering methodology there is a specific method of defining the functions.

Lawrence D. Miles defined a function in a unique way. He has devised a method of defining by two words. The first word is a verb and the second word is a noun. This unique definition has certain purpose. Value analysis/value engineering is a team approach. All the team members should think alike. This way of defining a function will give congruence of thought which is most important for the team. This is because if everybody thinks alike there will be a great help for creative solutions.

While the verb indicates what the item does, the noun describes what is to be accomplished without disclosing the method of accomplishment. The verb defines the required action from the item, i.e., it may generate, control, pump, etc. The noun must be measureable or at least understood in measurable terms, i.e., weight, load, decibels etc.

It advocates defining the use function in two words—an active verb and a measurable noun. This two-word definition will eliminate the ambiguity that may exist in sentences or a paragraph.

An active verb will indicate the action needed and the measurable noun will indicate the quantum.

A passive verb and a non-measurable noun define the selling function of the product, service or system.

As an example, the use function of a cup is to "hold liquid".

The verb "hold" indicates that some action is being done. The noun "liquid" may raise the question how much volume. This will force to think about the requirement of the customer. If it is felt that the requirement is less, then the volume of the cup can be reduced to that level.

The selling function of the cup is "improve appearance". This can be imparted to the item as per the need of the customer. When an item is from one segment to the next higher segment, this selling function gives a competitive edge to the item.

No two opinions about two words, but if an adjective, participle, or noun provides better understanding, then the third or fourth can be used. As an example,

- Adjective : Generates *electric* power
- Participle : Protects *recording* mechanism
- Noun : Measures *hydraulic* flow-rate

Charles W. Bytheway puts caution for the use of the extra word to make it more specific. The following quote will clarify.

"There is no set rule, but the fewer the modifier, the greater the opportunity to stimulate thinking and creativity because modifiers generally tend to restrict or narrow the scope of person's imagination, unless you have the ability to role-play." (Source: *FAST Creativity & Innovation* by Charles W. Bytheway, by J. Ross Publishing Inc)

A vocabulary of verbs and nouns is given in Table 2.1.

Table 2.1: Vocabulary of Verbs and Nouns

Work Function					
Verbs					
Absorb	Compress	Establish	Home	Modify	Rectify
Allow	Cut	Extrude	Interrupt	Prevent	Receive
Apply	Create	Emit	Insulate	Produce	Repel
Amplify	Collect	Eliminate	Impede	Protect	Route
Band	Conduct	Form	Induce	Plane	Support
Bake	Drill	Fire	Inspect	Roll	Shield
Change	Dry	Filter	Load	Restrict	Store
Control	Discard	Finish	Lift	Remove	Shape
Circulate	Dissipate	Grind	Module	Retain	
Cure	Drive	Generate	Move	Resist	
Convey	Enclose	Hold	Mill	Reduce	
Nouns					
Corrosion	Equipment	Heat	Protection	State	Weld
Current	Electricity	Insulation	Power	Saw	Warp
Circuit	Force	Light	Radiation	Transmit	Waste
Contamination	Flow	Liquid	Repair	Tap	Weight
Damage	Fluid	Motion	Supplies	Transport	
Density	Friction	Material	Sort	Torque	
Energy	Fixture	Oxidation	Spin	Voltage	

Sell Functions

Verb	Noun	Noun	Noun
Decrease	Appearance	Effect	Style
Improve	Beauty	Exchange	Symmetry
Increase	Convenience	Features	
Minimize	Decor	Form	
	Environment	Prestige	

The following is the list of functions where an extra word can be added as shown in Table 2.2.

Table 2.2: An Extra Word for Clarity

Function with Two Words	Functions with One Extra Word
Collect Data	Collect Warranty Data
Collect Data	Collect Accident Data
Construct System	Construct Mechanical System
Construct System	Construct Electrical System
Create Drawing	Create Detailed Drawing
Create Drawing	Create Assembly Drawing
Estimate Cost	Estimate Development Cost
Generate Power	Generate Mechanical Power
Generate Power	Generate Electrical Power
Generate Power	Generate Hydraulic Power
Issue Certificates	Issue Inspection Certificate
Measure	Air Flow
Measure	Hydraulic Flow
Protect	Protect Recording Mechanism
Protect	Protect Electronic Circuit
Protect	Protect Electric Circuit
Select Components	Select Mechanical Components
Select Components	Select Electrical Components
Train Employees	Train New Employees
Train Persons	Train Vendor Persons

2.5 EXERCISES ON FUNCTIONS

2.5.1 A screwdriver can be used in various ways. Convert the needs into function.

Need	Function**
To be used to a rotate screw	
To be used as a paperweight	
To be used to defend from enemy	
To be used to dig a hole	
To be used to open a lid	

** Answers are at the end of the chapter.

2.5.2 "When you get up in the morning and have breakfast, you may eat bread, butter and eggs along with a cup of tea or idly, dosa and a cup of coffee or alu-paratha with curd and a cup of milk, or if you are in hurry you may eat two bananas along with a cold glass of milk".

Can you state in two words what is described in the above sentence?

---------------------------------- ----------------------------------

Active Verb *Noun*

** Answer is at the end of the chapter.

2.5.3 Define the basic functions of the following items.

Items	Verb	Noun
Blast Furnace		
Arm Chair		
Electric Motor		
Spectacles		
Gas Tanks		
Canvas Roofs		
Car		
Life Insurance		
Copper Windings		

** Answer is at the end of the chapter

2.5.4 Define the functions of the following activities.

Activities	Functions	
	Verb	Noun
Establish/Selection criteria		
Respond to enquiries from customer		
Received emission data from test station		
Record emission data received from Test		
Make validation check		
Make QC check on the customer		
Check License application for emission compliance		
Issue pending letters		
Indicate reasons for denial		

** Answer is at the end of the chapter

2.5.5 After the random function analysis, the team should go into details. It may have to redefine the functions for getting the clarity. At the same time sometime what appears to be

a function is actually is an activity which should also to be corrected. The following exercise will help the readers to mature themselves in defining the function.

Unrefined Way		**Refined Way**	
Verb	**Noun**	**Verb**	**Noun**
Rotate	Shaft	Transmit	Torque
Hold	Bearing		
Paint	Casting		
Support	Blades		
Pump	Water		
Crush	Coal		
Maintain	Surface		
Maintain	Tolerance		
Maintain	Inventory		
Provide	Chromium plating		
Cut	Gear-teeth		
Provide	Doors		
Provide	Damp-proof layer		
Provide	Insulation		
Drill	Hole		
Mould	Bricks		
Construct	Tunnel		
Support	Roof		
Construct	Railway track		
Hold	Tie		

** Answer is at the end of the chapter

2.6 GUIDELINES TO IMPROVE FUNCTION IDENTIFICATION ABILITY

Some guidelines for improving function identification ability are listed below:

1. Use a dictionary and thesaurus for identifying the correct verb and noun.
2. Avoid using parts and operations as nouns. For example, "hold brush" should not be used as a function.
3. Never use functions like "meet specification," "improve safety". Instead use "assure cleanliness" and "protect operator" respectively.
4. Avoid the verbs provide, allow and facilitate. For example, the function of a water service line, instead of "provide service, use," transport water.

5. Do not use plural verbs, always use singular ones, for example, instead of "supports weight", use "support weight".
6. Do not use operations or activities as functions, for example, "drill hole" is an operation, "produce opening" is a function

2.7 TYPES OF FUNCTION

There are two types of function. They are:

1. Use function
2. Aesthetic or sell function

The purpose for which the customer needs the item is the use function. The use function of a pencil, in two words is to "make mark". If the pencil does not write, then it will not be able to perform its use function, and therefore will be rendered useless for the customer.

The function that fulfils the want of the customer is known as aesthetic function. It is those features of the item that provide aesthetic appeal to the item and help in selling the item. Aesthetic function is also called sell function. Only use function cannot help to sell the product. If you want to sell a pencil, then in addition to "make mark", its appearance, shape, etc. should be provided as per the desire of the customer segment. If the segment is school kids then pictures of Batman or Mickey Mouse will help to sell the product.

At this point I quote L.D. Miles,

"Many products and services require both use and aesthetic functions. Some require only use while some require only aesthetic functions. The refrigerator, automobile, dress, shoe, pipe and flower vase all require both use and aesthetic functions in varying ratios. The nail within the walls of the building, the concealed wire in the motor, and the oil in the automobile require only use functions. The "Rembrandt", the diamond, and the perfume have only aesthetic functions." (Source: *Techniques of Value Analysis and Engineering,* 2nd edition, McGraw Hill, New York, 1972 by Miles Lawrence D.)

Table 2.3: Use Function and Sell Function of a Product

Product	Use Function	Sell Function
Ornamental Jewellery	Beautify User	Display Brand
Bubble Packing Material	Absorb Shock	Reduce Weight
Car's Upholstery	Avoid Damage	Attract Customer
Gear Shift Lever	Engage Gear	Reduce Friction
Control Knob	Position Object	Indicate Rating
Navigation Display	Indicate Direction	Display Information
Battle Tank	Withstand Destruction	Improve Mobility
Water Storage Tank	Hold Water	Prevent Dirt
Colour Cement	Protect Surface	Improve Aesthetic
Briefcase	Enclose Parts	Enhance Image

2.7.1 In the following exercise, the name of the product is mentioned, indicate one use function (Basic) and one sell function.

Product	Use Function	Sell Function
Juicer		
Grinding Machines		
Iron Box		
Flower Vase		
Door Hinge		
Pulley Drive		
Toggle Switch		
Decorative Paints		

** Answer is at the end of the chapter

2.8 LEVELS OF FUNCTION

The functions of an item may be categorized into two levels. They are:

1. Basic function or primary function
2. Secondary function

Basic function of an item is that function for which the item comes into existence. If the function is eliminated but the item still exists, it is a clear indication that the selected function is not the basic function. For example, the basic function of an incandescent bulb is to produce light. If this function is eliminated there is no reason for the existence of the bulb.

Secondary functions are those functions that support the basic function. These functions are generated because of the specific design or the process adopted to achieve the basic function. To identify a secondary function, eliminate this function. If the component still exists, it is a secondary function.

Taking up the previous example, we know that an incandescent bulb produces heat in addition to light. If the function "produce heat" is eliminated, the component still exists. So we can conclude that "produce heat" is a secondary function.

The concept of identifying basic function and secondary function will be clearer with the following "Question – Answer – Conclusion" Dialogue., in Table 2.4.

Table 2.4: Incandescent Bulb

1	Function being considered	Produce light
	Logic question	If "produce light" is eliminated will the purpose be satisfied?
	Answer	No
	Conclusion	Produce light is a basic function
2	Function being considered	Produce heat
	Logic question	If "produce heat" is eliminated will the purpose be satisfied?
	Answer	Yes, it will
	Conclusion	Produce heat is a secondary function

2.9 METHOD OF FINDING THE FUNCTIONS OF A PRODUCT

A product may be a single item product like a spanner or may be an assembly of various items like a screwdriver which is having items like handle, blade, pin, etc. In both the cases, the product will have a basic function as well as a number of secondary functions.

To enumerate the various functions, the following steps have to be adhered to:

Step 1: The primary question to be asked to the product as a whole is "What does it do?" In answer to this question, there will be a number of functions. All those functions have to be defined in two words, i.e., a verb and a noun.

Step 2: Basic function out of all the functions as in step (1) will be selected using the logic mentioned in Table 2.4. All other functions will be the secondary functions of the product as a whole.

Step 3: Dismantle the product into sub-assemblies or components.

Step 4: If there are sub-assemblies, then consider each one as a unique product and identify the basic function and the secondary functions as per steps (1) and (2).

Step 5: Dismantle the sub-assemblies into components. Each component will become a single item product; identify the different design features of the product.

Step 6: Applying steps (1) and (2) identify the basic functions as well as secondary functions of all the components. The existing design features are to be considered one by one to find out the functions.

Step 7: Make a summary of all identified functions against each component or feature.

2.9.1 Case History

In order to illustrate how to define the functions of a product, a very common item is taken, which is being used everyday, that is, a cup, as shown in Fig. 2.1 below.

Fig. 2.1.

Function analysis will be fruitful if an individual or the team has an adequate information of the project which may be a product or process or system. When the team is working on some live project then that information is available through adequate data collection. But when an individual starts function analysis one should also have sufficient knowledge about the product. Now, we have a best teacher which is the Internet. Through this you gain sufficient information about the project.

Based on that concept, the following information has been collected for the "mug" of our project which is as below.

2.9.2 Historical Details of Mug

A mug is a cup that was designed for drinking hot beverages, such as coffee, tea, hot chocolate or soup. Mugs have handles and hold a larger amount of fluid than other types of cup. On an average a mug holds about 12 ounces (350 mL) of a liquid but the size varies greatly due to the large variety of mugs available. A mug is a less formal style of drink container compared to the cups used in a coffeehouse. It is the cup most often used at home for casual use and is not often found in a formal setting.

Historically, mugs were often carved in wood or bone or shaped of clay. Today modern mugs are made with ceramic materials such as earthenware, bone china, porcelain, or stoneware. Some are made from strengthened glass, such as Pyrex. Technically, porcelain mugs are just one category of ceramic mugs and the difference between them is due partially to the content, partially to the manufacturing process, and partially by the ideas that people have put into them.

The design of the mug is made for thermal insulation to keep the contents warm. The thick walls of a mug insulate the beverage from the air and keep it from cooling too quickly. The bottom of the mug is not flat but concave to give it space from conducting any temperature from the surface on which it sits. The mug is taller than it is wide to lower the amount of the drink open to the air that could cause it to cool. Mugs are larger in volume than many other cups making a thermodynamic shape an important aspect of the design.

Coffee mugs are often plentiful in many a cabinet in most peoples homes. They have become an item that is sold everywhere from gift stores to coffee shops to supermarkets. They are being used as an object for promotion and advertisement. This is because the coffee industry is a multi billion dollar industry. Four million dollars is spent on imported coffee to the U.S. each year with 100 million coffee drinkers a day.

Coffee mugs are sold in a wide variety of locations. Companies such as Starbucks, eBay, Amazon, and other smaller businesses are places where mugs are bought both online and from the stores. There are now businesses offering "create-your-own-mug," customised mugs, and other personalized mugs as the coffee mug industry had become a popular item for a gift.

2.9.2.1 *General Design and Functions*

Much of the mug design aims at thermal insulation: the thick walls, as compared to the thinner walls of teacups, insulate the beverage to prevent it from cooling or warming quickly. The mug bottom is often not flat, but either concave or has an extra rim, to reduce the thermal contact with the surface on which a mug is placed. These features often leave a characteristic O-shaped stain on the surface. Finally, the handle of a mug keeps the hand away from the hot sides of a mug. The small cross section of the handle reduces flow heat between the liquid and the hand. For the same reason of thermal insulation, mugs are usually made of materials with low thermal conductivity, such as earthenware, bone china, porcelain or glass.

Handles can often be afterthoughts. They are put on at the end of the manufacturing process and, at that point, many potters are ready to move on to the next stage. But they are important elements, both functionally and aesthetically, so they should get the attention they deserve.

(Source from INTERNET)

Step 1: What does a mug do? The answers in the form a verb and noun are:

- Contains liquid
- Resists temperature

- Withstands load
- Accommodates fingers

Step 2: The function that is identified as the basic function is "contain liquid". If "contain liquid" is eliminated will the purpose be satisfied? Answer is "no." Hence, it is a basic function.

Step 3: The cup has two components, that is:

- Body
- Handle

Step 4: Is not relevant in this case because there is no sub-assembly.

Step 5: The features of the existing design of the body are:

- Shape
- Dimension
- Material
- Texture
- Printing

Step 6: The functions of the body are defined in two words. To facilitate the process, function identification can be done against each existing design features of the body.

Step 7: The features of the second component are:

Handle

- Material
- Dimension
- Texture

The feature-wise functions of the body and handle are given in Table 2.1. Table 2.1 also indicates the basic function.

Table 2.5: Feature - Function Matrix

Components	**Feature**	**Details of feature**	**Function**		**Types (B/S)**
			Verb	**Noun**	
Body	Shape		Contain	Liquid	B
					S
	Dimension	Diameter	Produce	Shape	S
		Height	Produce	Shape	S
		Bottom curvature	Reduce	Thermal conduction	S
		Thickness	Produce	Shape	S
			Reduce	Heat-flow	S
	Material	Bone China	Reduce	Thermal conduction	S
			Join	components	S
			Withstand	Load	S

Contd.

Table 2.5: Contd.

Components	**Features**	**Details of Feature**	**Function**		**Types (B/S)**
			Verb	**Noun**	
			Withstand	Thermal stress	S
	Texture		Attract	Customer	S
	Printing		Convey	Message	S
Handle	Dimension	Curvature	Produce	Shape	B
			Accommodate	Finger	S
			Reduce	Heat-flow	S
		Elliptical Cross section	Reduce	Heat-flow	S
	Material	Bone China	Reduce	Thermal conduction	S
			Join	Components	S
			Withstand	Load	S
			Withstand	Thermal stress	S
	Texture		Attract	Customer	S

Summary of functions of a mug are shown in Table 2.2.

Table. 2.6: Summary of Functions

Sr. No.	**Functions**		**Related to which components**	
	Verb	**Noun**	**Body**	**Handle**
1	Contain	Liquid	Yes	–
2	Produce	Shape	Yes	Yes
3	Reduce	Thermal Conduction	Yes	Yes
4	Withstand	Load	Yes	Yes
5	Attract	Customer	Yes	Yes
6	Convey	Message	Yes	–
7	Accommodate	Finger	–	Yes
8	Reduce	Heat-flow	Yes	Yes
9	Join	Components	Yes	Yes
10	Withstand	Thermal Stress	Yes	Yes

2.10 ASPECTS OF FUNCTIONS

2.10.1 Function as a Communication Tool

The two-word definition of a function provides the congruence of thought process. This can be used to express the need, wants and desire of the

FAST of MUG

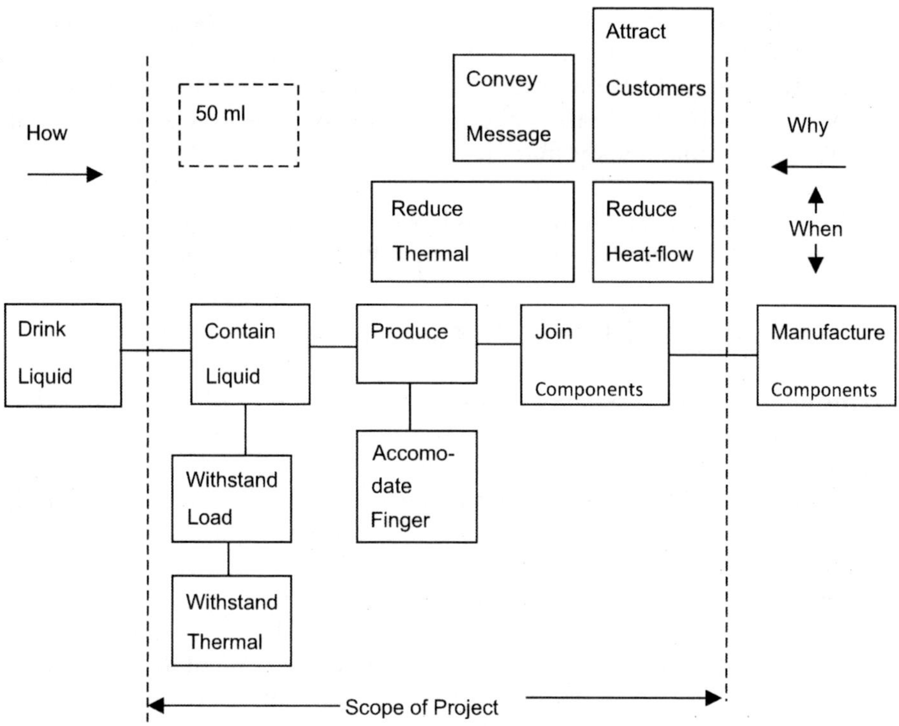

customer. "Circulate air" is the need of the item. "Indicate constituents" is the want for the customer for any food item. "Improve aesthetic", the color of the bumper of a car is the desire of the owner.

2.10.2 Function can Expose Misunderstanding

Definition of function will help to eliminate the misunderstanding. An example will clarify that. In my class I take up the example the most common item, that is, a screwdriver. Almost everybody some time or the other uses this item. Even that when I ask the question that what is the function of the tip of a screwdriver. The invariable answers are:

- Hold screw
- Screw bolt
- Drive screw
- Tighten/loosen screw
- Rotate screw, so on.

It will continue without coming to the point. In order to change the direction of their thinking, I said that if the thickness of the tip is thick what will happen. They immediately came with the idea that it will not fit in the slot. Then, what is the function of the tip? Now they started saying that it is "fix slot". Now, the noun is correct. Is the verb correct? Participants did not agree to that. Then again I said if the tip is thin then what will happen? They said it will not be able to rotate the screw. Then what should be the verb? It should be active. Now some of the member came out spontaneously that "it will be suit". Hence, the function of the tip is "suit slot".

It was agreed by all that though they were using screwdiver for quite some time, their understanding about the item was not proper.

2.10.3 Functions will Reveal Misconception

During a practice session of defining the function of different objects, one of the objects was 'calculator". Some participants said that the function of a calculator is to "solve problem". This was not agreed by some participants. They came out with the idea that the function is "follow command". When it was thrown to all, everybody accepted the second definition.

But why is this difference? It is because the first group of participants did not have a fair idea about the calculator while the second group had a fairly clear conception of the working of the calculator. Unless one gives proper instructions, it will not give the correct result.

2.10.4 Function can be a Nucleolus of Creativity

The item for the practice of function was an "armchair". Various definitions emerged out, like:

- Provide comfort
- Rest body
- Facilitate sitting
- Give relaxation
- Comfort sitting

It was asked if you come and sit in a chair and it breaks then what will happen. Think the function of the armchair in the light of the incidence. After quite a long deliberation the participants agreed to "support human". When the question was asked that for what part of the human the chair is required, the answer came as "weight". Hence, the final definition agreed by all was "support weight".

Now, the question is how a proper definition will help one to be creative. It was said that the "support weight" will be the same whether the armchair is for a kid, or for an adult or for the board- room. If the armchair meant for a kid with an average weight of fifteen kilograms and the chair is manufactured for the average weight of twenty-five kilograms, then it is clear that unnecessary cost has crept in and which can be eliminated. In other case if it is buckled with the weight of ten kilograms, then also it is clear that it is having less value to the customer and can be improved. Had the definition of the armchair been accepted as "provide comfort", this information would not have been available and the team would face difficulties to improve the product.

2.10.5 Function: A Gateway to Major Breakthrough

The breakthrough solution can only be achieved when you work on function. If you concentrate on the parts, you will be able to improve the product marginally that too with enormous effort. But if you choose the needed functions and develop the product, the product will be a value added product.

Thomas Alva Edison is an example. Had he tried to improve the lantern he would have got a better lantern. But instead of that he concentrated with the function of "produce light" and so he came out of the product like "incandescent bulb". If you trace the product development history, you will find that the breakthrough has come through concentrating on needed functions. (17. 9. 2008)

2.10.6 Function and Activity

In the function analysis of hardware, one has to come to the lowest level, that is components and their functions have to be identified. But the lowest level of any procedure or system is activities and one has to find out function of those activities. Hence, it is essential to know the difference between function and activity.

The function is the objective or purpose whereas the activity is the method of achieving that purpose.

2.11 RULES TO CHECK CORRECTNESS OF FUNCTION DEFINITION

Rule No. 1

Check for good verbs. Avoidable verbs are: provide, allow, facilitate, ensure

Rule No. 2

Nouns should be measureable

- Should have unit, like kg, decibel, etc. for work function
- Sensitivity to art & beauty for sell function

Rule No. 3

Does the function elicit creativity?

For example: not "make tunnel" but "produce passage"

Rule No. 4

Verb should not be plural

- Should be "support weight"
- and not "supports weight"

Rule No. 5

Check whether operations or activities are used as functions.

- "Drill hole" is an operation
- "Produce opening" is a function

Rule No. 6

Correct definition reduces tension

(I have observed during value study that if the correct definition has not been arrived, it irritates. When the correct definition is found it releases the tension.)

ANSWERS

2.5.1 A screwdriver can be used in various ways. Convert the needs into functions.

Need	Function
To be used to rotate screw	Transmit Torque
To be used as paper weight	Secure Items
To be used to defend from enemy	Protect Individual
To be used to dig a hole	Produce Opening
To be used to open a lid	Remove Cover

2.5.2 "When you get up in the morning and have breakfast, you may eat bread, butter and eggs along with a cup of tea or idly, dosa and a cup of coffee or alu-paratha with curd and a cup of milk, or if you are in hurry you may eat two bananas along with a cold glass of milk".

Can you state in two words what is described in the above sentence?

Supply	*Nutrients*
Active Verb	*Noun*

2.5.3

Items	Verb	Noun
Blast Furnace	Produce	Heat
Armchair	Support	Weight
Electric Motor	Produce	Torque
Spectacles	Correct	Vision
Gas Tanks	Possess	Volume
Canvas Roofs	Produce	Shade
Car	Transport	Weight
Life Insurance	Buy	Security
Copper Windings	Generate	Magnetic Fluxes

2.5.4 Define the functions of the following activities.

Activities	Functions	
	Verb	**Noun**
Establish/Selection Criteria	Establish	Criteria
Respond to enquiries from customer	Notify	Customer
Received emission data from test station	Receive	Result
Record emission data received from Test	Enter	Result
Make validation check	Validate	Record
Make QC check on the customer	Validate	Test
Check license application for emission compliance	Verify	Compliance
Issue pending letters	Indicate	Non-Compliance
Indicate reasons for denial	List	Infractions

2.5.5

Unrefined Way		Refined Way	
Verb	**Noun**	**Verb**	**Noun**
Rotate	Shaft	Transmit	Torque
Hold	Bearing	Locate	Parts
Paint	Casting	Resist	Corrosion
Support	Blades	Support	Weight
Pump	Water	Increase	Head
Crush	Coal	Reduce	Size
Maintain	Surface	Maintain	Dimension
Maintain	Tolerance	Maintain	Interchangeability
Maintain	Inventory	Minimize	Downtime
Provide	Chromium plating	Increase	Life
Cut	Gear-teeth	Obtain	Shape
Provide	Doors	Secure	Access
Provide	Damp-proof layer	Exclude	Moisture
Provide	Insulation	Prevent	Accident
Drill	Hole	Produce	Opening
Mould	Bricks	Obtain	Shape
Construct	Tunnel	Create	Passageway
Support	Roof	Support	Weight
Construct	Railway track	Aid	Movement
Hold	Tie	Retain	Position

2.7.1

Product	Use Function	Sell Function
Juicer	Crush Object	Satisfy Senses
Grinding Machines	Maintain Tolerance	Prevent Accident
Iron Box	Enclose Items	Secure Customer
Flower Vase	Accommodate Objects	Improve Aesthetic
Door Hinge	Swing Object	Attract Customer
Pulley Drive	Transmit Torque	Increase Longevity
Toggle Switch	Make/Break Contact	Reduce Friction
Decorative Paints	Reduce Corrosion	Create Distinction

2.12 EXERCISE

1. **Write down the primary and secondary functions using the verb and noun conventions for the following items.**
   (a) LCD Projector (b) Fruit Juicer
   (c) Thermos Flask (d) Pulley
   (e) Road Median (f) Hexagonal Bolt
   (g) Paper Clip (h) Adhesive Paper

Identify the part or component that performs the work function and the selling function in the above listed items.

(IEB 5 Innovation and Value Engineering, January 2007)

2. **"Work functions are defined using a measurable noun and actionable verb". Explain the need for this convention, taking the following examples to illustrate.**
   (a) Current (b) Torque
   (c) Volume (d) Energy Conversion

(*IEB 5 Innovation and Value Engineering, IIIE, Section B, January 2007*)

3. **What is the basic function of "rice"**
   (a) Satisfy Hunger (b) Fill Belly
   (c) Provide Energy (d) Supply Carbohydrate

4. **What is the basic function of "water"**
   (a) Avoid Dehydration (b) Eliminate Thirst
   (c) Supply Solvent (d) Fill Stomach

5. **What function is not:**
   (a) A communication tool (b) Remove misconception
   (c) Remove misunderstanding (d) An activity

6. **The basic function of "sieve" is:**
   (a) Segregate Size (b) Remove Dust
   (c) Differentiate Item (d) Clean Items

7. **The basic function of an "engine" is:**
   (a) Produce Heat (b) Produce RPM
   (c) Produce Torque (d) Produce Force

8. **There are two basic functions of the "ear"**
   (a) Receive Sound
   (b) Improve Look
   (c) Maintain Body Balance
   (d) Differentiate between Animals

9. Some verbs should always be avoided. Choose two answers.
(a) Produce (b) Ensure
(c) Conduct (d) Provide

10. How many words define a function
(a) One (b) Two
(c) Three (d) Four

11. How to define a work function?
(a) Measurable noun followed by a passive verb
(b) Non-measurable noun followed by an active verb
(c) Active verb followed by a measurable noun
(d) Measurable noun followed by an active verb

12. What does verb indicate?
(a) What the item does (b) How the thing is done
(c) Measure of work content (d) No specific indication

13. What are the questions in function phase?
(a) What is it? How is it being done? Who does it?
(b) Where it has been done? What is it? What does it do?
(c) What must it do? What is it? Who does it?
(d) What is it? What does it do? What must it do?

14. Can an aesthetic function become a basic function?
(a) Yes (b) No

15. A component can have only one function.
(a) Yes (b) No

16. Define the work functions and sell functions using the verb and noun for the following items.
(a) Juicer (b) Grinding machines
(c) Iron box (d) Flower vase
(e) Door hinge (f) Pulley drive
(g) Toggle switch (h) Decorative paint
(*IEB 5 Innovation and Value Engineering; Section B; August 2010*)

CHAPTER

3

Fundamentals of Function Analysis System Technique (FAST)

"Just knowing what something costs can save five percent. Improvements in material can save 10 percent, but finding a better way can save 30 percent or more. FAST and the FUNCTION STRUCTURE both can help approach and surpass the 30 percent. Let's face facts and make maximum use of the tools we have available to us rather than expending time to confuse the issue."

— *Carlos Fallon*

3.1 LIFE OF CHARLES W. BYTHEWAY

Charles W. Bytheway was born on 13th February, 1926. He graduated from the University of Utah in mechanical engineering in 1952. He did his Master of Science in mechanical engineering in 1961 from the same university. He received his value engineering certificate from the University of California in Los Angeles in 1960.

His interest areas were designing, building and improving the existing things. He designed heating and air-conditioning systems for Lennox Industries Inc. and also designed mining equipment for EIMCO Corporation. He joined Sperry Rand Corporation where he designed a turret during the Vietnam War. He conducted his first value engineering seminar in 1960 in the Sperry Rand Corporation.

Charles W. Bytheway introduced the methodology of Function Analysis System Technique (FAST) to the Society of American Value Engineers (SAVE) at their International Conference in 1965.

Until retiring in 1981, Bytheway served as the Director of Value Engineering in Salt Lake City. Then he went to work for the Salt Lake Community College in its mechanical engineering department. He became an associate professor in that department.

He published nineteen papers on FAST Diagramming and other related subjects. Other than value engineering and FAST Diagramming he combined the four gospels of one New Testament into a single gospel text which was published in 1988.

Bytheway was the first recipient of the Lawrence D. Miles Award by the Society of American Value Engineers, presently known as SAVE International for his FAST Diagramming. He is a certified value specialist and a Fellow of SAVE International.

Charles W. Bytheway is a devout follower of the Church of Jesus Christ of latter-day saints, and served a mission in New Zealand for twenty-seven months and has served in bishoprics and other ecclesiastical positions of leadership within his church for the past 45 years.

He was married to the former Frieda Duehlmeir. They have four daughters and two sons, twenty-three grandchildren, and two great granddaughters.

3.2 GENESIS OF FAST

The change from the beaten path is always responsible for coming out with a new thing. It was true also with Charles W. Bytheway.

Charles W. Bytheway was working with Sperry Rand Corporation in Salt Lake City, Utah. The company decided to open a value engineering department. Bytheway was requested to take a temporary assignment in a value engineering seminar. Till that time he had minimal exposure to value engineering. He joined the Value Engineering class in the University of California, Los Angeles. This was the first ever class on Value Engineering in the University.

The instructor used the Job Plan developed by L.D. Miles. He started talking about function. Bytheway learnt to define a function in two words: an active verb followed by a measurable noun. It was new to him. To put it in his words, "The function concept fascinated me."

After coming back to his organization he started conducting value engineering workshops. At that time there was no method of identifying the basic function. So Bytheway developed a method of his own to find out the basic function. It was observed by many, specially his boss C.S. Grey that Bytheway could generate a lot of creative ideas.

One day C.S. Grey said to him, "It works for you but it doesn't work for anyone else because we don't know how you think." Grey again said, "Why don't you write down how you think!"

On his request, Bytheway started thinking what actually he was doing and he came to a conclusion that he used two-question techniques. They were "how" and "why" to all the functions and thereby tried to build a relationship between the functions.

He then decided to name his technique and came up with the name: Functional Analysis System Technique. But he realized that there was already a mathematical technique with the name of Functional Analysis, so he called his technique as Function Analysis System Technique (FAST).

Sometime I feel, C.S. Grey was the prime mover of FAST because he had forced Bytheway to put his thoughts on paper, otherwise we would have lost that forever.

3.3 PROCESS OF FUNCTION ANALYSIS

The process of function analysis can be put diagrammatically (Fig. 3.1).

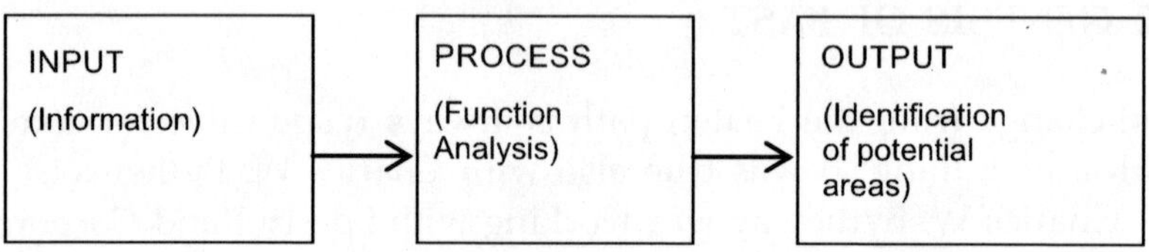

Fig. 3.1.

Input

The input is the information gathered by the team members. It is an initial and the most vital point. The output depends on the proper information from the correct source.

Process

Function Analysis may be done in the following ways.

- Function Cost Worth Analysis
- Functional Analysis System Technique (FAST)
- Function Cost Allocation

Output

The output of the process is the identification of potential areas. They may be as below:

- Functions which require improved performance.

- Functions where cost reduction is possible without reducing the performance.
- Functions which have no value from customers' point of view and can be eliminated.
- Functions which have some value but are expensive.

3.4 PRINCIPLES OF FAST DIAGRAMMING

Charles W. Bytheway developed the concept and methodology of FAST Diagramming. He used the 'ladder" concept in horizontal format. The basic two deterministic questions were: "how" and "why". The "how" logic is applied from the left to the right and the "why" logic from the right to the left. While answer to the "how" logic is the solution, the answer to the "why" logic is the requirement.

In the FAST Diagramming, each function is put in a block and the blocks with the function inside are put after the question "how" and "why". So, against each function two more functions will generate, one from the question "how" and the other from the question "why". This can be shown in the following diagram:

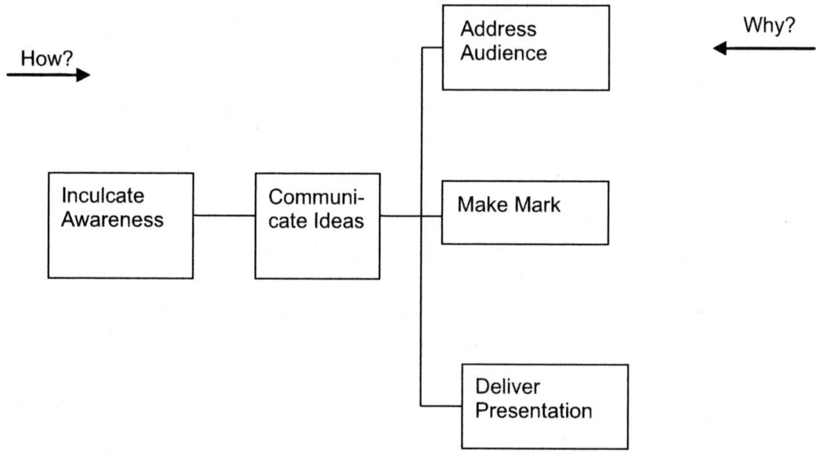

Fig. 3.2

Let us start with the function "communicate ideas". When one asks the question "why", to the "communicate Ideas", the answer will be the requirement for that function. That means what is the objective for communicating the ideas. Here, the answer comes to "inculcate awareness". But when one asks the question "how" the answers may be many like—"make mark", "address audience", or "deliver presentation". One can check whether the logic is okay or not, by asking the question "why" to all functions. It is possible that the answer in all cases will be to "communicate ideas".

Each of the three functions namely, "address audience", "make mark" and "deliver presentation" may be the basic functions of three different types of products (concepts). They are speeches, pencil, and presentation. The questions of "how" will be applied to one of the basic functions and one will get one new function. This new function has to be validated through the logic of "why" and the process will continue. "Functions leading to concepts" is shown in Table 3.1.

Table 3.1: Functions Leading to Concepts

Highest Order	Higher Order	Basic	Concepts
		Address Audience	Personal Voice, Collar Mike, Hanging Mike, Public Address System, etc.
Inculcate Awareness	Communicate Ideas	Make Mark	Chalk, Pencil, Dot Pen, Fountain Pen, etc.
		Deliver Presentation	Blackboard, Flip Chart, Over Head Projector, Power Point Techniques, etc.

Now let us look to the three functions, namely "inculcate awareness", "communicate ideas" and "address audience", and what is the relationship among them. The right hand function is the lower order function compared to the immediate left hand function. So, "address audience" is the lower order function compared to "communicate ideas". Similarly, "communicate ideas" is the lower order function in comparison to "inculcate awareness".

Similarly, the left hand function is the higher order function in comparison to the left hand function. In this example "communicate ideas" is the higher order function in comparison to "address audience" and "inculcate awareness" is the higher order function in comparison to "communicate ideas".

The father of FAST Diagramming, Charles W. Bytheway had developed nine questions which helped him to find out the various things he wanted to know. These are enumerated in Table 3.2.

Table 3.2: Charles W. Bytheway's Logical Questionnaire

Sr. No.	Questions	Logic
1.	What subject or problem we would like to discuss (two-word function)?	
2.	What are we really trying to do when we have the (two-word function)?	
3.	What higher order function has caused it (two-word function) to come into being?	**Higher Level**
4.	Why is it necessary to have it (two-word function)?	
5.	Why is it necessary to have it (two-word function)?	
6.	How is (two-word function) actually accomplished or how is it proposed to be accomplished?	**Critical Path**
7.	Does the method selected (two-word function) caused any supporting functions to come into existence?	
8.	If we don't have (two-word function), would we still have to perform the other functions listed?	**Basic Function Determination**
9.	When we have (two-word function) in the manner conceived, does it cause the apparent dependent functions to come into existence?	
10.	What or who actually (two-word function)?	

3.5 UTILITY OF FAST

The concept of FAST Diagramming came into being almost after two decades of invention of the concept of value engineering. It was said that there were two types of function, one is basic and the other is secondary. The basic function is that for which the item has been created and the secondary functions are those which support the basic function. But there was no method available to really identify the basic function. If the item is small where there is less number of functions it is possible to identify the basic function but when the functions increase it is a difficult task to do so. Arthur E. Mudge tried to solve the problem by using paired comparison method. But that also could not satisfy the value engineers' requirements. They wanted something more which could give more pointed focus to the basic function.

Not only was identification of the basic function important but there was no relation also between the functions. The functions were identified randomly and then analyzed through function-cost—worth analysis to find the value gap. There was no method to identify whether all the functions had been identified and/or they had been properly defined.

It was not clear what the need of the customer was. Is it what we have perceived? Or is it something else?

The FAST Diagramming helped one to become creative. When one asks the question "how", he may get a number of ideas which can be crystallized through creative thinking and then one can choose the best course of action. In this connection I quote Thomas J. Snodgrass and Muthiah Kasi as below:

".... One can easily understand how various freedom fighters fulfilled the function, **secure freedom. Social leaders** advocated passive resistance and non-violence protest to *secure freedom*. **Presidents** of countries tried to *secure freedom* for other countries by direct involvement or through arms sales. **Guerrillas** tried to *secure freedom* by staging civil war against the authorities. **Terrorists** struck against anybody to *secure freedom*. Four extremely different methods perform one function."

A similar situation exists in the industries also. FAST Digramming will help to pinpoint the real need of the customers and not the perceived need. The advantages of FAST can be enumerated as below:

- It can be used as a communication tool.
- It will be able to refine functions generated randomly.
- It will stimulate creativity of the team members.
- It may be used as a tool to check missing functions.
- It will be able to identify the basic function(s).
- It will exclude unnecessary functions from the rest of the functions.

The utility of FAST Diagramming is that it answers all the questions which were not answered previously. Creating an item without FAST Diagramming is like moving around without any purpose.

3.6 COMPARISON AMONG PERT, CPM AND FAST

The objectives of PERT/CPM are:

- Both are activity oriented.
- Optimization of resources through proper scheduling.
- Assisting in a scientific identification and planning of various activities.
- Physical assessment of performance in terms of time and resources.
- Efficient management and control of the process of implemen-tation of the project.

The main differences in these two techniques are:

- PERT is based on probabilistic estimates, that is, through using PERT one can estimate the probability of completion of the project.

- CPM is based on deterministic logic.
- CPM techniques are used in maintenance projects, regular construction jobs where time estimates are fairly accurate.
- PERT techniques are applicable in projects of research and development where accurate estimation is not possible.

Function Analysis System Technique is a systematic diagramming technique that logically identifies and visually displays the necessary function to accommodate a design purpose.

FAST is a function oriented diagram. The main logic is used in FAST are "how?" and "why?" In addition to that FAST is also used in "when" logic.

3.7 TYPES OF FAST

There are three different types of FAST Diagramming. They are:

- Basic FAST Diagramming
- Technically Oriented FAST Diagramming
- Customer-Oriented FAST Diagramming

3.8 EXERCISE

1. **What is the utility of a FAST diagramming tool?**

   (*IEB 5 Innovation and Value Engineering, IIIE, Section B; January 2007*)

2. **Elaborate the principles of FAST Diagramming with an example of your choice.**

3. **Encircle the correct answer**
   (a) The creator of FAST is Arthur E. Mudge
   (b) The creator of FAST is Muthiah Kasi
   (c) The creator of FAST is L.D. Miles
   (d) The creator of FAST is Charles W. Bytheway

4. **The answer of "how" (?) logic:**
   (a) Is the basic function
   (b) Is the higher order function
   (c) Is the lower order function
   (d) Does not lead to anything.

5. **Who was the motivator of Charles W. Bytheway to write down his thoughts?**

(a) C.S. Grey (b) Arthur E. Mudge
(c) L.D. Miles (d) Carlos Fallon

6. **What was the original name proposed by Bytheway?**
   (a) Final Analysis System Technique
   (b) Functional Analysis System Technique
   (c) Function Analysis System Technique
   (d) Formal Analysis System Technique

7. **The answer of "why" (?) logic:**
   (a) Is the required secondary function
   (b) Is a one time function
   (c) Is the lower order function
   (d) Is the higher order function

8. **The answer of "how" (?) is the requirement**
   (a) True (b) False

9. **The answer of "why" (?) is the solution.**
   (a) True (b) False

10. **There is no unique FAST diagram. It varies from person to person and also on the philosophy of different teams.**
    (a) True (b) False

11. **Which phase is recommended for the application of FAST?**
    (a) Audit phase (b) Evaluation phase
    (c) Function phase (d) Creative phase

12. **Which statement is not an advantage of FAST?**
    (a) It will stimulate the organization.
    (b) It will be able to refine functions generated randomly.
    (c) It can be used as a communication tool.
    (d0 It may be used as a tool to check missing functions.

13. **In a maximum of two paragraphs (about 8 to 10 sentences) clarify the meaning and purpose of the following statement.**
    "Function Analysis System Technique is a useful representation of the functional logic of the product systems"
    (IEB 5 Innovation and Value Engineering; Section B; February 2009)

14. **Who was the first recipient of the Lawrence D. Miles Award by the Society of Value Engineers?**
    (a) Arthur E. Mudge (b) Carlos Fallon
    (c) Charles W. Bytheway (d) J.J. Kaufman

15. Charles W. Bytheway had developed questions which helped him to find out the various things he wanted to know. These are:

(a) 6 (b) 7
(c) 8 (d) 9

16. "The process in making the diagram is important, not the perfection of the resulting diagram". The above statement is

(a) Unacceptable (b) Accepted
(c) Rejected (d) Not sure

17. What are the benefits of representing functional information in a FAST diagram? Explain the advantages with the help of an example.

(IEB 5 Innovation and Value Engineering; Section B; July 2005)

CHAPTER

4

Basic (Classic) FAST Diagram

*"**FAST** reduces the time for complex analysis. One diagram may be worth more than many times one thousand words. It can be understood and appreciated by almost anyone. One Pennsylvania agency produced an agency plan by another method which required 638 pages. **FAST** would produce a more comprehensive and meaningful plan using less than 50 pages!"*

– Donald P. Goss, Director,
Bureau of System Analysis
Commonwealth of Pennsylvania,
Harrisburg, Pennsylvania

4.1 INITIATION OF FAST DIAGRAMMING

There are a lot of activities before starting to draw the FAST Diagram. Each and every step is important and needs to be followed religiously. So it needs elaboration of each step. The steps may be put as below:

- Project selection
- Team selection
- Random function definition
- Function spreadsheet

4.1.1 Project Selection

Project selection is the most important part of value methodology. Proper selection may yield maximum return on investment (ROI). Unless the project is given by the management, it needs a lot of care to select a value engineering project.

As soon as the project is finalized, the team should start collecting all the cost data. They should also collect the various data like production problems, maintenance problems, customer complaints, etc. These are important because this information may help to come out with ideas which can take care of the challenges identified.

4.1.2 Team Selection

The process of FAST Diagramming is a team effort. It requires selecting proper team members. The proper selection will help in generating new ideas which will help to come out with a cost-effective and innovative solution.

In the format of basic FAST model, there are three areas. The area at the right side of the scope line, the second one is scope area of the project and the third portion is the area of the left side of the scope line.

As per J.J. Kaufman, CVS, a well known educator of FAST Diagramming, the team members should be selected from the above-mentioned three areas.

If the team selection is for the project related to real estate, the member from the right side area after the scope line could be someone from the sales/marketing department. The members from the scope of the project area could be civil engineers, architects, finance experts, etc. The member from the left side of the scope line could be one of the top management personnel of the organization.

If it is an engineering project, the members from the input area, which is from the right side, could be from the sales & marketing department. The members from the scope area could be from the engineering department and from the output that is the left area from the left scope line could be the production manager.

4.1.3 Random Function Definition

4.1.3.1 Product

In order to understand this, it is better to illustrate it with an example. Let us select a very common item—a "shaving brush". The photographs of the shaving brush in assembled condition along with components are shown in Fig. 4.1 below. Red rubber band is not a part of the shaving brush. It is used to keep it in a bunch.

The random function definition process can be streamlined into a structured process to get better results and achieve a comprehensive coverage of function identification. If it is an assembly, the next level will be sub-assembly. Then from the sub-assembly one should go to the component level. Then, one should progress from the component level to the features level. This procedure will help to identify not only the

Fig. 4.1. Shaving Brush Assembly and Its Components.

items but their special features. In our example of "shaving brush" there is no sub-assembly. Hence, one can go straight to the components. The components of a shaving brush are shown in Fig. 4.1:

1. Bristles
2. Bunch of bristles
3. Handle
4. Seal cap
5. Expander
6. Resin

To define the function the following format should be used.

Table 4.1: Function Identification

Item	Functions		Features
	Verb	**Noun**	
Bristles	Facilitate	Handling	Flexibility of bristles
	Ensure	Comfort	Bristle curvature
	Grant	Leverage	Length of bristles
	Optimize	Length	Length bristles
	Create	Bunch	Number of bristles

Bunch of bristles	Hold	Water	Bunch of bristles
	Ensure	Comfort	Spherical shape of bunch
	Develop	Lather	Length of the bunch of bristles
Resin	Secure	Bristles	
Handle	Accommodate	Bristles	Top hole in the handle
	Facilitate	Grip	Handle profile
	Identify	Manufacturer	Printed logo
	Improve	Appearance	Color and shape
	Accommodate	Cover	Bottom hole
	Stabilize	Position	Outside diameter
Cover	Prevent	Impurities	Activity of the cover is to restrict impurities
Expander	Expand	Bristles	Expanding lower part of the bunch of bristles

4.1.3.2 Process

The same random identification should be done for the process also. Let us think of a simple process which everybody is familiar with. The process may be thought of as below:

"The process of watering the garden."

Problem

Debashis Mukherjee is sitting on his porch at his New York house, and he decides to water the garden. He leaves the porch, walks to the garage at the other end of the house, opens the garage door, and walks to the tool locker. There he lifts the reel of the garden hose from the locker, carries it to the rear garage door, opens it, and carries the hose to the faucet at the rear of the garage. He attaches the hose to the faucet, and begins to water the garden.

The activity has been put in Table 4.3. To find the functions of each activity ask the question "what does 'activity' do?" Remember that the activity is the method of achieving the purpose, but the function is the purpose.

Table 4.2: Process Analysis

Travel in Feet	Symbol	Activity Description	Explanation
85	→	To garage door	He leaves the porch walks 85 ft to garage door. This is called transportation, since he moves from one place to another.
	(1)	Opens door	Opening the garage door is an operation.
10	→	To tool locker in garage	He walks 10 ft to locker to get hose. A transportation
	(2)	Removes hose from locker	This is an operation
15	→	To rear garage door	He carries hose to rear garage door. A transportation
	(3)	Opens door	This is an operation.
10	→	To faucet at rear of garage	This is transportation.
	(4)	Attaches hose to faucet and opens faucet	This is considered one operation
	(5)	Water garden	He begins the main operation of watering garden

Table 4.3: Function Identification

Activity	Process	Function	
		Verb	Noun
To garage door	What does 'activity' do?	Fetch	Components
Opens door	What does 'activity' do?	Make	Way
To tool locker in garage	What does 'activity' do?	Cover	Distance
Removes hose from locker	What does 'activity' do?	Unclamp	Component
To rear garage door	What does 'activity' do?	Cover	Distance
Opens door	What does 'activity' do?	Make	Way
To faucet at rear of garage	What does 'activity' do?	Cover	Distance
Attaches hose to faucet	What does 'activity' do?	Deliver	Water
	What does 'activity' do?	Join	Components
Opens faucet	What does 'activity' do?	Allow	Water
Water garden	What does 'activity' do?	Moisten	Soil

4.1.4 Function Spread Sheet

4.1.4.1 Product

In order to find out the relationship between the functions, one of the best ways is to use "function spreadsheet". In this method one can use both the deterministic logic, namely, "how" and "why". By using this one can develop the relationship between the functions.

The procedure of using "function spreadsheet" is as below.

Put each identified function from the random functions identification on the central column of the spreadsheet one by one. Ask the question "why" to that function and write those functions on the left side column. Then ask the "how" question to the central column function. The answer that comes out from that should be put on right side column. The functions that come out from the above two questions should be expected to be from the random identified functions. This method will help to redefine the function to have proper relationship between the functions. This will also help one to find out the missing functions. It is not necessary that all the functions will be required for the model.

The function spreadsheet is given in Table 4.4.

Table 4.4: Function Spread Sheet for Product

← Why How →

Function	Function	Function
	Facilitate Handling (Independent Function)	Facilitate Grip
	Ensure Comfort (Independent Function)	Grant Leverage
Ensure Comfort	Grant Leverage	Optimize Length
Develop Leather	Hold Water	Create Bunch
Smoothen Skin	Develop Leather	Hold Water
Create Bunch	Secure Bristles	Accommodate Bristles
Secure bristles	Accommodate Bristles	Make Mould
Facilitate handling	Facilitate Grip	Produce Uneven Surface
Confirm Quality	Identify Manufacturer	Mark Name
Increase Sale	Improve Appearance	Incorporate Feature
Secure Bristles	Accommodate Cover	Make Mould
	Facilitate Handling (Independent Function)	Stabilize Position
Hold Water	Create Bunch	Secure Bristle

4.1.4.2 Process

A function spreadsheet can also be drawn for a process. The method of preparing is the same. In our case it can be drawn as below.

Table 4.5: Function Spreadsheet for a Process

← Why How →

Function	Function	Function
Moisten soil	Deliver water	Allow water
Deliver water	Allow water	Join components
Allow water	Join components	Collect components

4.2 MODUS OPERANDI OF FAST DIAGRAM

The basic FAST format, also known as classic FAST diagram is credited to Charles W. Bytheway. The details of the format are shown in Fig. 4.2.

All the terms of the format will be elaborated to have more clarity.

4.2.1 Scope Line

There are two scope lines, one at the left side of the diagram and the other on the right side of the diagram. The peculiarity of the scope line is that it is a dotted line. The basic function of this scope line is to limit the scope of the project in question.

Another important aspect of the left scope line is that the function on the right side of this line is the basic function which is inside the scope area. Similarly, the function on the left side of the line is the higher order function.

The right scope line is the limit of the project. The function on the right side of the line is the causative function (assumed function). It is also known as lower order function.

4.2.2 How (?), Why (?) and When (?) Logic

The FAST Diagram is drawn based on deterministic logic. The question of "how (?)" and "why (?)" logic is used for developing this diagram. "How" logic will have to be followed from the left side of the left scope line to the right side and the "why" logic will be followed from the right side of the right scope line to the left side. "When" logic will indicate when that function happens.

4.2.3 Higher Order Function (HOF)

The higher order function is the objective of the project. This is also considered the output of the project under study. The higher order

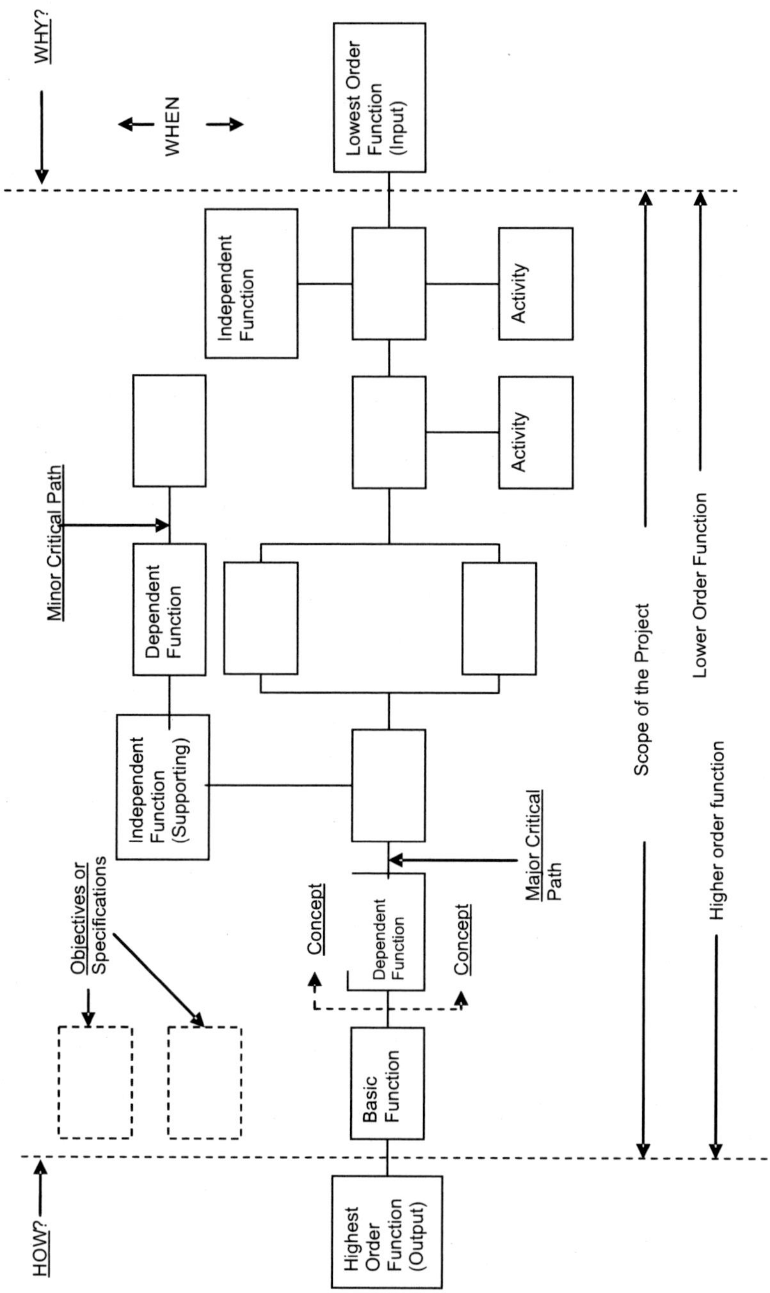

Fi.g. 4.2. The Basic FAST Model (Classic).

function is derived from asking "why (?)" question to the basic function. It is also thought of as the requirement of the management. The clarity of this function is essential; otherwise it may lead to a wrong or sub-optimal solution. It is placed on the left side of the left scope line.

4.2.4 Lower Order Function (LOF)

The lower order function is regarded as the input to the project under study. It is placed on the right side of the right scope line. This function is not a part of the project. This is also known as causative function, assumed function. "Why (?)" question to this function will leads to a function which is a part of the study. It is important to identify this function during the formulation of FAST Diagram.

4.2.5 Basic Function

The place of the basic function is the right side of the left scope line. "How (?)" question of the higher order function will lead to the basic function. It is already known that the basic function is that function for which the project comes into existence. A knowledgeable person of FAST Diagramming can pinpoint the basic function without knowing anything about the project. This diagramming method clarifies the doubt of finding out the basic function of the project.

4.2.6 Concept

The concept is an indication that from this point the functions on the right side will be based on the particular design approach. With an example the point can be clarified.

The basic function of a "fountain pen" or "pencil" is to "make mark". If one adopts a design aspect as "fountain pen", then the functions after "make mark" will be different than if the design approach is "pencil'. It will be further different if one adopts a design approach as "ball point pen".

The concept point is shown by arrows both at the top and the bottom indicating the right-hand side.

4.2.7 Objectives or Specifications

The specialty of this block is that it is made of dotted lines. This is not a function, but this is the objective(s) of the design concept. The position of this block is above the basic function block. There may be more than one block, based on the requirement. It may be used for specifications also. Once it is finalized the team has to work towards that.

4.2.8 Major Critical Path Functions

The functions which satisfy the "how (?)" and "why (?)" logic are connected by a straight line. This straight line path is known as the major critical path and the functions which are on this line are called major critical path functions. These functions are only responsible to achieve the objective. These functions come into being because of a certain design concept. Change of the design concept will change the functions on the major critical path other than the basic function and higher order function which are parts of the major critical path.

4.2.9 Independent (or Supporting Function) Functions

Independent functions are those functions which are not dependent on any other function. When it follows the "when" logic in relation to some other function and if it is a function, it will be placed in the top of the major critical path as an independent function. Dependent function of this independent function will follow a minor critical path.

4.2.10 Dependent Functions

The dependent functions are the right hand functions in comparison to the left hand functions. These are true for both major and minor critical path functions.

4.2.11 Minor Critical Path Functions

If there is a dependent function of the independent function, then it will follow a path which is called minor critical path. In other words, in the minor critical path the end function is an independent function. This path will also follow the "how (?)" and "why (?)" logic.

4.2.12 Function

The function is the objective or purpose of doing any job.

4.2.13 Activity

The activity is the method of achieving the purpose. The activity connected with a function with "when" logic is placed on the lower part of the major critical path in the diagram.

4.3 STANDARDIZATION OF DRAWING FAST DIAGRAMMING

To draw a FAST Diagram one needs to have a standardized approach, so that everybody will understand what each symbol means. This was initiated by J.J. Kaufman. Standardization of FAST Diagramming and his standardized method is as below.

4.3.1 Deterministic Logic

In the FAST diagramming, the placement of functions is based on deterministic logic. These deterministic logics are "how (?)"; "why (?)" and "when (?)". This is depicted in Fig. 4.3.

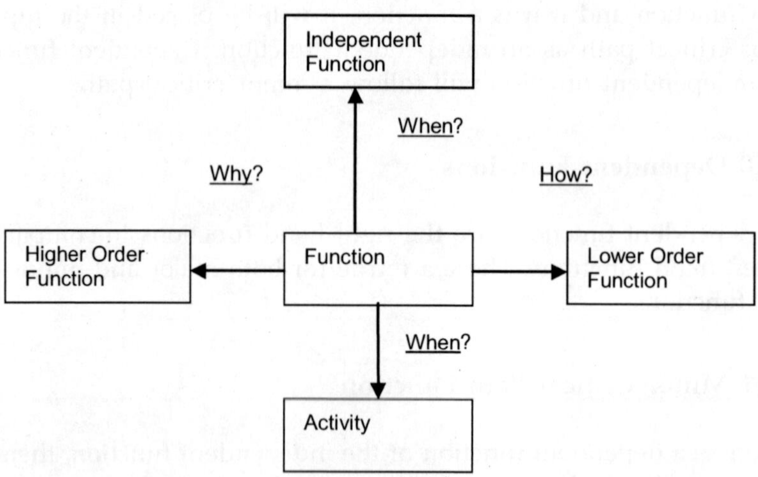

Fig. 4.3. Deterministic Logic.

4.3.2 "And" (Equal Importance)

The symbolic representation of functions of equal importance are shown in Fig. 4.4.

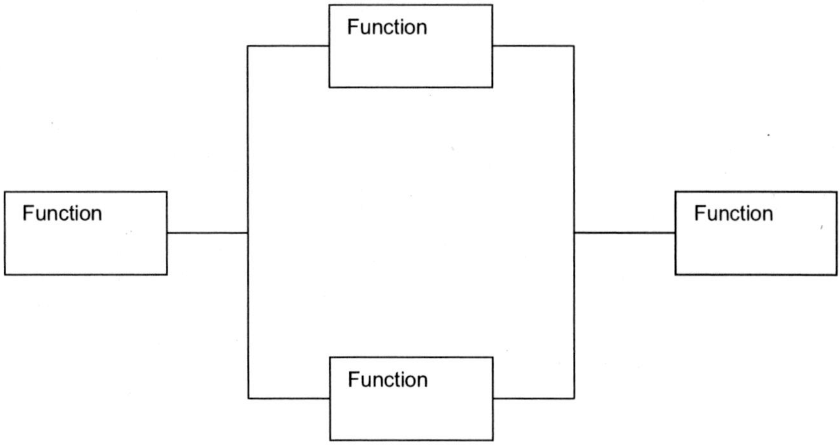

Fig. 4.4. "And" (Equal Importance).

4.3.3 "And" (Less Importance)

The symbolic representation of functions of less importance are shown in Fig. 4.5. Less important function has been put below.

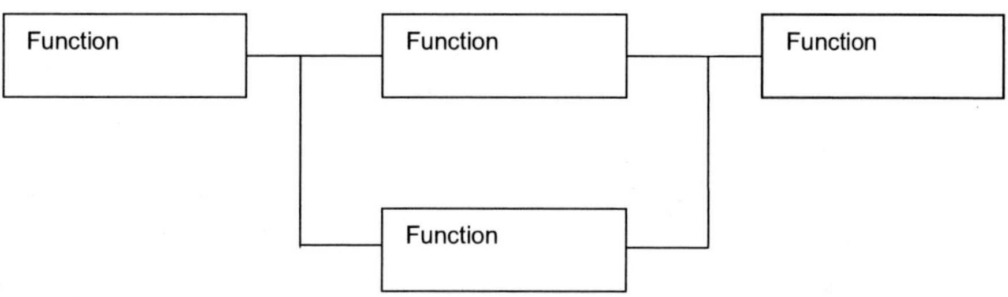

Fig. 4.5. "And" (Less Importance).

4.3.4 "Or" (Equal Importance)

The symbolic representation of "Or" (equal Importance) is shown in Fig. 4.6.

4.3.5 "Or" (Less Importance)

The symbolic representation of "Or"(less Importance) is shown in Fig. 4.7. Less important function has been put below.

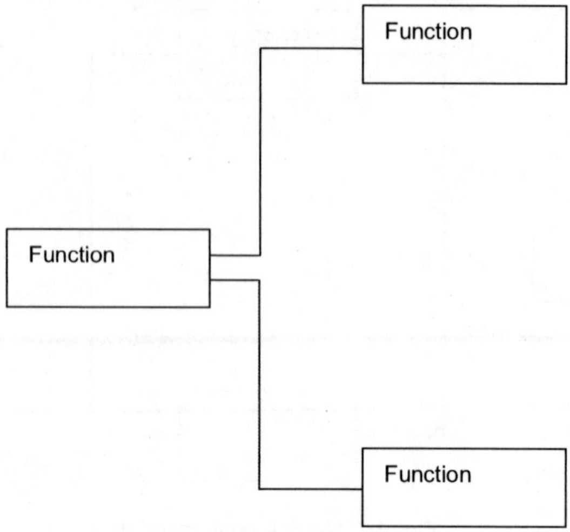

Fig. 4.6. "Or" (Equal Importance).

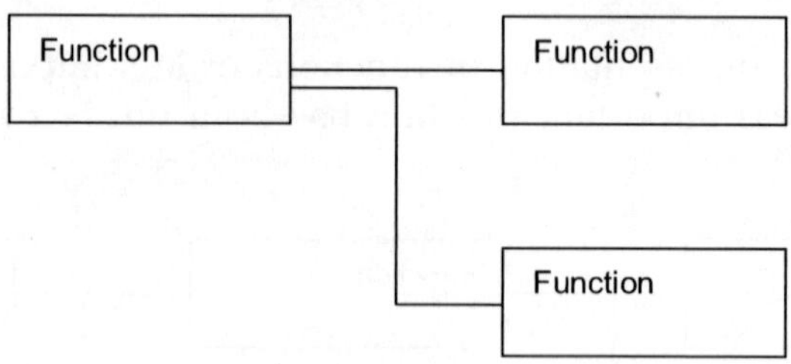

Fig. 4.7. "Or" (Less Importance).

4.3.6 "And" Along the "When" Direction

The independent function should be placed in the "when" direction above the major critical path. The function which is nearer to the critical path is more important than the function which is away from the major critical path. This is shown in Fig. 4.8.

4.3.7 "And" along the "When" Direction

The activity should be placed in the "when" direction below the major critical path. The activity which is nearer to the critical path is more important than the other activity which is away from the critical path. This is shown in Fig. 4.9.

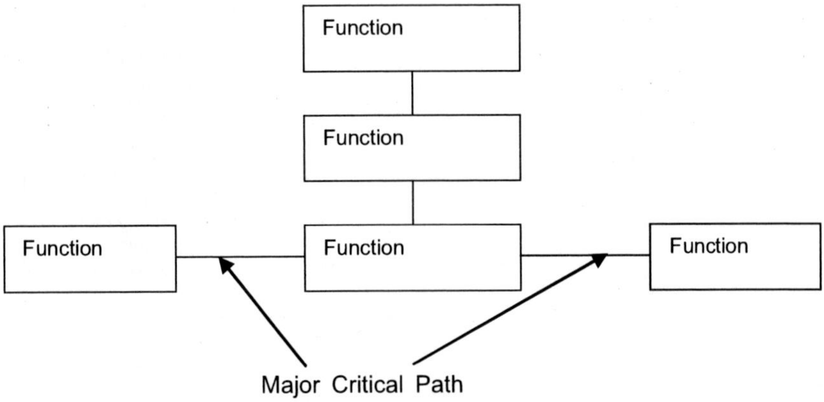

Fig. 4.8. "And" along the "When" Direction.

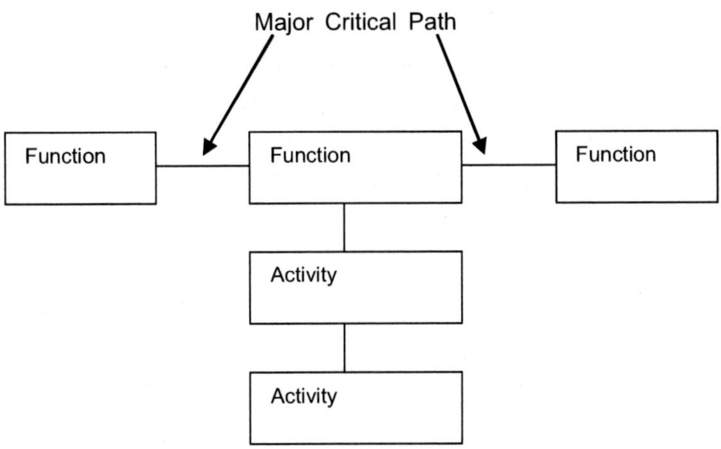

Fig. 4.9. "And" along the "When" Direction.

4.3.8 "Or" along the "When" Direction

The symbolic representation of this situation when it is towards the independent function is depicted in Fig. 4.10.

4.3.9 "Or" along the "When" Direction

The symbolic representation of this situation when it is towards the activity is shown in Fig. 4.11.

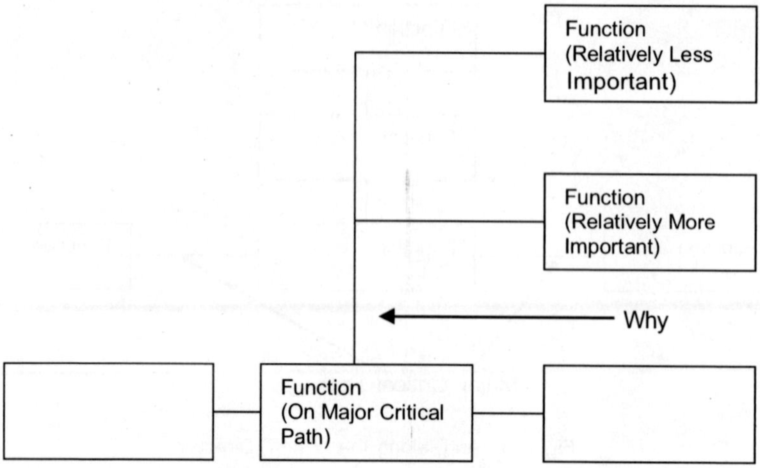

Fig. 4.10. "Or" along the "When" Direction.

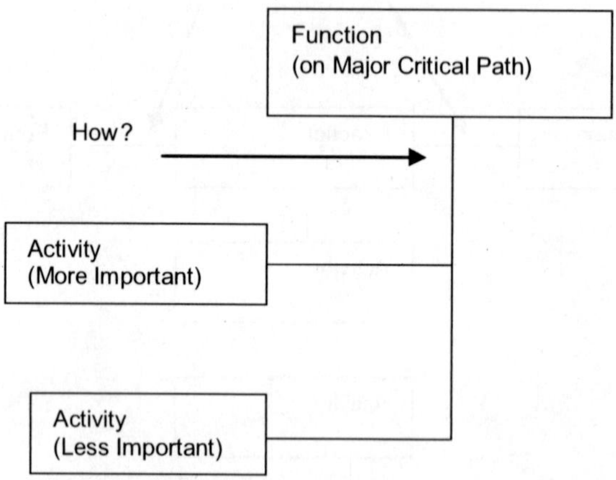

Fig. 4.11. "Or" along the "When" Direction.

4.3.10 Other Notations and Symbols

<u>**A**</u> indicates the continuation of network, but the team may not be interested. <u>**B**</u> indicates that function (F) is further expanded on a lower level of abstraction and <u>**C**</u> indicates that the line connects elsewhere on the model matching the same number **(X)** are shown in Fig. 4.12.

4.4 HOW TO DRAW A FAST DIAGRAM

The drawing of a FAST diagram is a matter of practice. More one draws the diagram it will be clearer. It needs practice. But one should know how to proceed for drawing a FAST Diagram. There is nothing

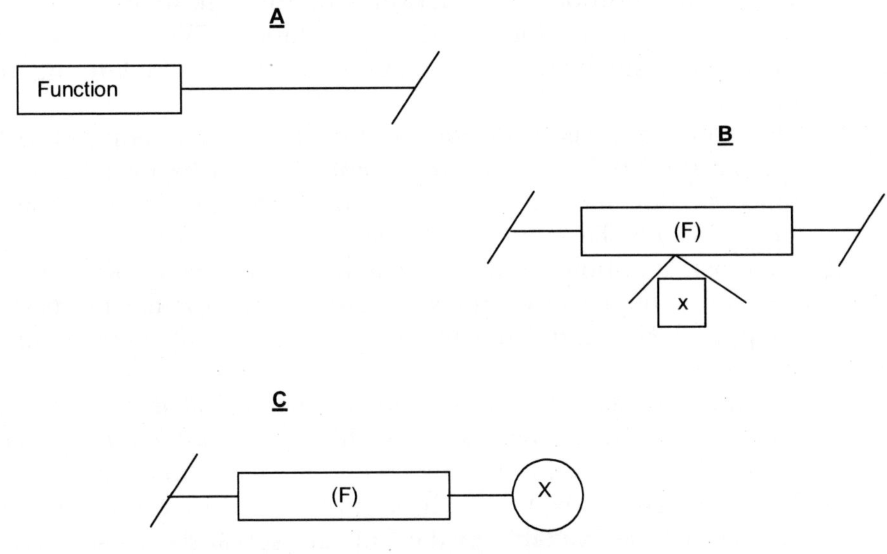

Fig. 4.12.

like a correct FAST. It is the concept of the user and it may be different in different situations. The only thing is to follow the rules of drawing the FAST Diagram. The following are the steps for drawing a FAST Diagram.

1. It should be a team effort.
2. At least one of the members should know about the project thoroughly.
3. It will be useful if one of the members is not a technical person. The benefit comes from this is that someone has to explain the pros and cons of the project. While doing that a lot of clarifications will happen about the project itself.
4. All the members should know about value methodology.
5. Initially, the team should start with the function definition of the project as a whole in two words.
6. Then the project, if it is a product, should be divided into the sub-assembly, components, and features. If it is a process, it should be divided into sub-processes; activities and if it is a system then, it should be divided into sub-systems; activities and procedure.
7. Now, the functions are to be defined in two words—an active verb and a measurable noun.
8. Write down each function in small "Post-it™" notes. This is used because you can put it at one place and can shift to another at will.

9. The team should use function spreadsheet to develop the relationship among the functions developed. This will also help to develop some missing functions as well as redefining the function.
10. The team now has to decide the function which "appears to be a basic function". The starting point can also be by taking any function. But, the author always advocates for identification of "appears to be basic function" first.
11. Now ask question "why" to that function. The answer of that function is higher order function. This function is not the part of the project. Hence, this function will not be available in the random functions list.
12. The higher order function should be finalized at this stage. This will be done by asking "how" to this higher order function and get it validated by questioning "why" to "basic function".
13. The next step will be to ask "how" to the same basic function. The answer will be available in the function spreadsheet itself. Write that function on the Post-it notes and place it to the right side of the basic function.
14. Now all the three functions are connected with the "how" and "why" logic.
15. Now proceed from left to right with "how" logic and fix them on the same line.
16. When that is completed verify those functions with the "why" logic from right to left.
17. Now draw a left hand scope line after the basic function. It should be a dotted line. Outside the dotted line the higher order function will be there.
18. In the right side there will be the function which is not a part of the project. Put before that function on the left side a dotted scope line which is the right side scope line.
19. Confirm that the left side function of the right side scope line should be a part of the project.
20. When the critical line functions are finalized, the team has to find out which function is an independent function. The function has to find out when that function happens. Then that function will be put above that function.
21. At this position the team can use the function spreadsheet and come out with any function which follows the "how" & "why" route of this independent function.
22. If there is any function that should be placed in the right side of the independent function.
23. With the logic of "how" and "why", the minor critical path can be established.

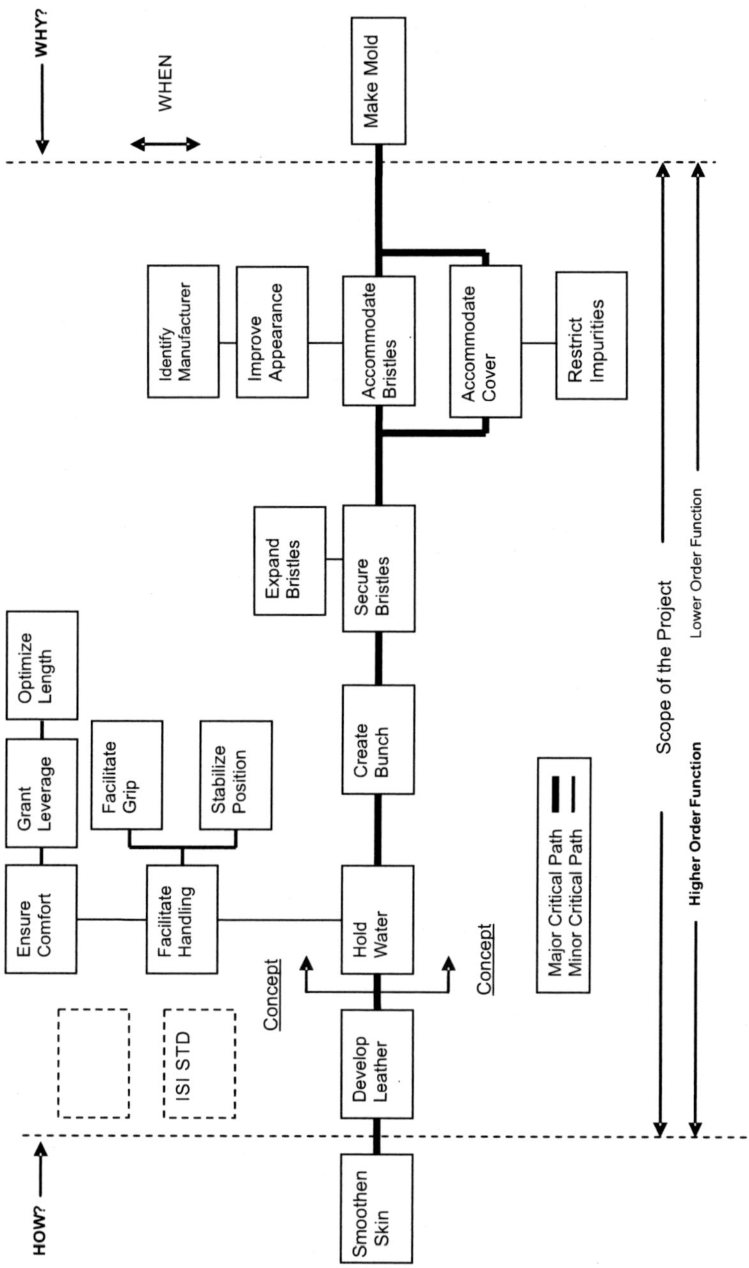

Fig. 4.13. FAST Diagram of a Shaving Brush (CLASSIC).

24. The team with the same procedure can establish if there is any other minor critical path.
25. If there is any activity which happens at the same time of any function, it will be placed under that function.
26. The design objectives of the project are placed above the basic function. The blocks for the design objectives are made of dotted line. It is to be remembered that the design objectives are not functions. Hence, it will not be available in the random functions list.
27. Since all the functions are on "Post-it" notes, these can be moved if the team feels so.
28. When the team finalizes the diagram it should be copied and drawn in the workbook.

4.5 ILLUSTRATIONS

4.5.1 Product

The basic FAST diagram for the shaving brush which has been dealt with earlier is shown in Fig. 4.13.

4.5.2 Process

The basic FAST diagram for watering the garden which has been dealt earlier with is drawn in Fig. 4.14.

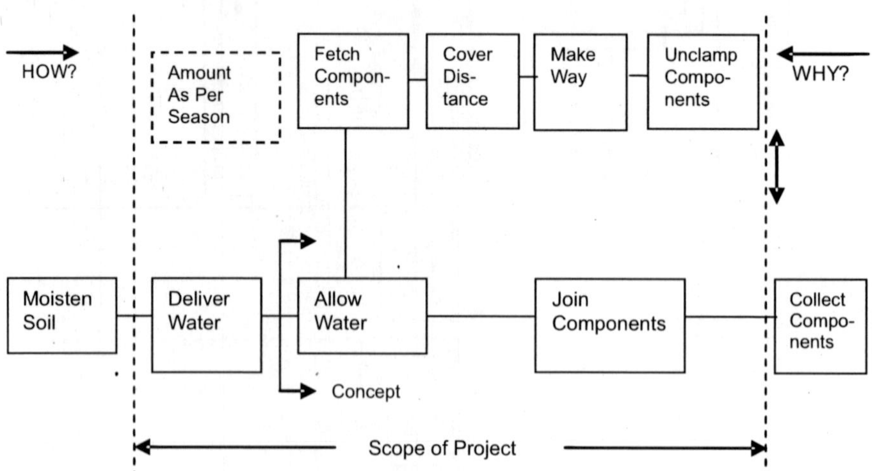

Fig. 4.14. FAST Diagram of Watering the Garden (CLASSIC) .

4.6 EXERCISE

1. **What are salient features of a basic (Classical) FAST diagram? Draw the format of basic FAST model.**

2. **Encircle the correct answer out of the four given below. What are the deterministic logics used in basic FAST model.**
   (a) Who, Where and Whom (b) Where, When and What
   (c) How, Why and When (d) How, Where and When

3. **Encircle the correct answer out of the four given below. The scope lines will indicate:**
   (a) Area of the project (b) Scope of the project
   (c) The place for functions (d) Nothing

4. **The creator of basic (Classical) FAST is**
   (a) Arthur E. Mudge (b) J.J. Kaufman
   (c) T.J. Snodgrass (d) Charles W. Bytheway

5. **In the basic FAST model, which path is there?**
   (a) Medium critical path (b) Higher critical path
   (c) Minor critical path (d) Optimum critical path

6. **Which is the place dedicated for the "Function In Question" in the function spreadsheet**
   (a) Left place (b) Centre place
   (c) Right place (d) Can be placed anywhere

7. **Which activity is not necessary for initiation of FAST diagram?**
   (a) Top executive meeting (b) Project selection
   (c) Team selection (d) Random function definition

8. **Which item is not there in the basic FAST model?**
   (a) Basic function (b) Major critical path
   (c) Independent function (d) One time function

9. **Which item is unique in basic FAST model?**
   (a) Higher order function (b) Basic function
   (c) Concept direction (d) Lower order function

10. **Where is the "activity" placed in the basic FAST model?**
    (a) Top of basic function
    (b) On the major critical path
    (c) On the minor critical path
    (d) Under the function on major critical path

11. The symbol of item A in the Fig. 4.15 is

(a) And (equal importance) (b) Or (equal importance)

(c) Or (less importance) (d) And (less importance)

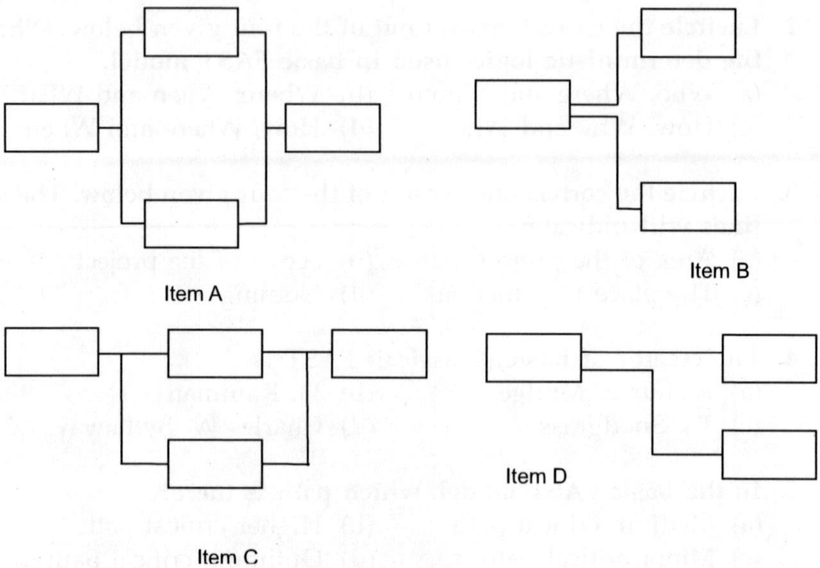

Fig. 4.15.

12. The symbol of item B in Fig. 4.15 is

(a) And (equal importance)

(b) Or (equal importance)

(c) Or (less importance)

(d) And (less importance)

13. The symbol of item C in Fig. 4.15 is

(a) And (equal importance) (b) Or (equal importance)

(c) Or (less importance) (d) And (less importance)

14. The symbol of Item D in Fig. 4.15 is

(a) And (equal importance) (b) Or (equal importance)

(c) Or (less importance) (d) And (less importance)

15. The "independent function" is placed at which place of major critical path.

(a) Bottom (b) Middle

(c) Side (d) Top

16. From the major critical path most important independent function is placed

(a) Away (b) Far away
(c) Nearer (d) Nothing specific

17. The "activity" is placed at which place of major critical path

(a) Bottom (b) Middle
(c) Side (d) Top

18. From the major critical path most important activity is placed

(a) Far away (b) Nearer
(c) Away (d) Nothing specific

19. What is "X" in item A in Fig. 4.16?

(a) Secondary function (b) Basic function
(c) Independent function (d) Lower order function

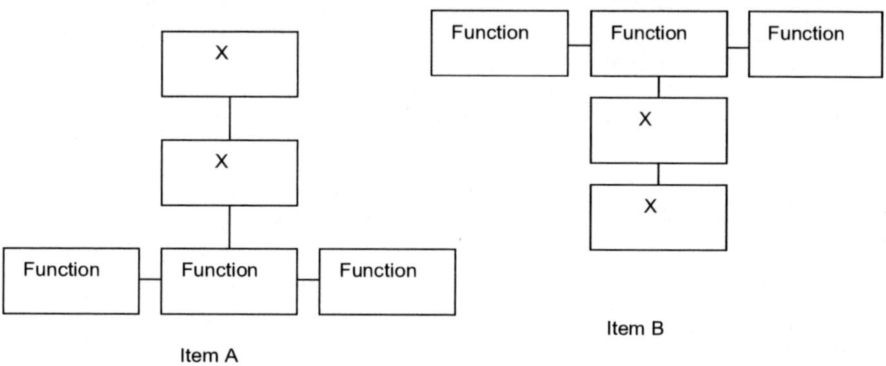

Fig. 4.16.

20. What is "X" in item B in Fig. 4.16?

(a) Secondary function (b) Activity
(c) Independent function (d) Dependent function

CHAPTER

5

Technically Oriented FAST Diagram

"The ***FAST Diagram*** *... clarifies a problem and pinpoints the area to apply creativity. It then helps to sell the idea by providing a concrete plan to demonstrate and guide discussion."*

— Richard Park, Manager, Value Control, Chrysler Corporation, Detroit, Michigan.

5.1 MODUS OPERANDI OF FAST DIAGRAM

The format of Technically Oriented FAST Diagram is shown in Fig. 4.1. While there are a lot of similarities between Basic FAST and Technically Oriented FAST, a lot of dissimilarities exist between them too. Moreover, there is a distinct difference in approach in drawing the Technically Oriented FAST Diagram. The author feels it is necessary to elaborate all the aspects of Technically Oriented FAST, even if it appears to be a repetition.

5.1.1 Scope Lines

The scope lines are made of dotted lines; it is same as in the basic model. Two scope lines enclose the scope of the project. The left side is known as left scope line while the right one is the right scope line.

5.1.2 How (?), Why (?) and When (?) Logic

The FAST Diagram is drawn based on deterministic logic. The questions of how (?) and why (?) logics are used for developing this diagram. The "how" logic will have to be followed from the left side of the left scope line to the right side and the "why" logic will be followed from the right side of the right scope line to the left side. "When" logic will indicate when that function happens.

5.1.3 Higher Order Function

The higher order function is the objective of a value engineering project. It should be defined in two words and is not a function of the project in question. The higher order function should be in a block of full lines and should be placed on the left side of the left scope line.

5.1.4 Basic Function

The basic function is the function for which the product or process or system is created. The dedicated place for the basic function is on the right side of the left scope line. The higher order function and the basic function should be linked with a line (not arrow). The answer to the question of "why" to the basic function should be the higher order function. Similarly, the answer of the question "how" of the higher order function should be the basic function. If this logic does not hold good, then there must be some problem, like, missing some function in between the higher order function and the basic function or wrong definition of function.

5.1.5 Required Secondary Function

The question "how (?)" to basic function will lead to another function. Similarly, the next question of "why (?)" will be asked to this new function. The answer should be the basic function. If it happens and is accepted by the members then it is the correct function and in the correct place. This function is connected with the basic function by a line (not arrow). This new function is called "required secondary function".

Now if you ask again the question "how (?)", one will get another function. This new function again has to be asked "why (?)" question. If the answer is first required secondary function, then it is the second required secondary function of the project. This required secondary function will be connected with the first by a line (not arrow).

This process will have to continue till one finds that the function accepted is not a part of the project.

5.1.6 Lower Order Function / Causative Function / Assumed Function

The last function which is not a part of the project will be the first function beyond the right side scope line. This function is known as the lower order function. This is also known as the causative function or assumed function. This function is connected with the last required secondary function by a line (not arrow).

The lower order function is the input to the project under consideration.

5.1.7 Critical Path

The blocks containing higher order function, basic function, required secondary functions and the lower order function are connected by lines (not arrows). This line is known as the critical path. One of the indications of the critical path is that it contains those functions which are related to each other by the deterministic logic "how (?)" and "why (?)".

The functions on the critical path are the only functions which can provide the objective, that is, higher order function and these are the only essential functions. As an empirical rule the number of functions in the critical path should not be more than four to five (Muthiah Kashi).

5.1.8 Design Objectives

The design objectives are those norms which have to be followed while working on a project. When one is doing on the existing product, they have to assume what are those norms which had been taken into account to create the existing one. If it is a new thing, then the team has to decide the norms based on which the things will be developed.

The design objective is not a function, hence not a part of the project. The design objective can be more than one.

The allocated place in the diagram is above the basic function. The block should be made up of dotted lines. Design objective should not be connected with the basic function by any line or arrow.

5.1.9 One-time Functions

These functions are unique in nature. It happens only once in the life cycle of the product/process/system. Based on that characteristic those are termed "one-time functions". The allocated place for these types of

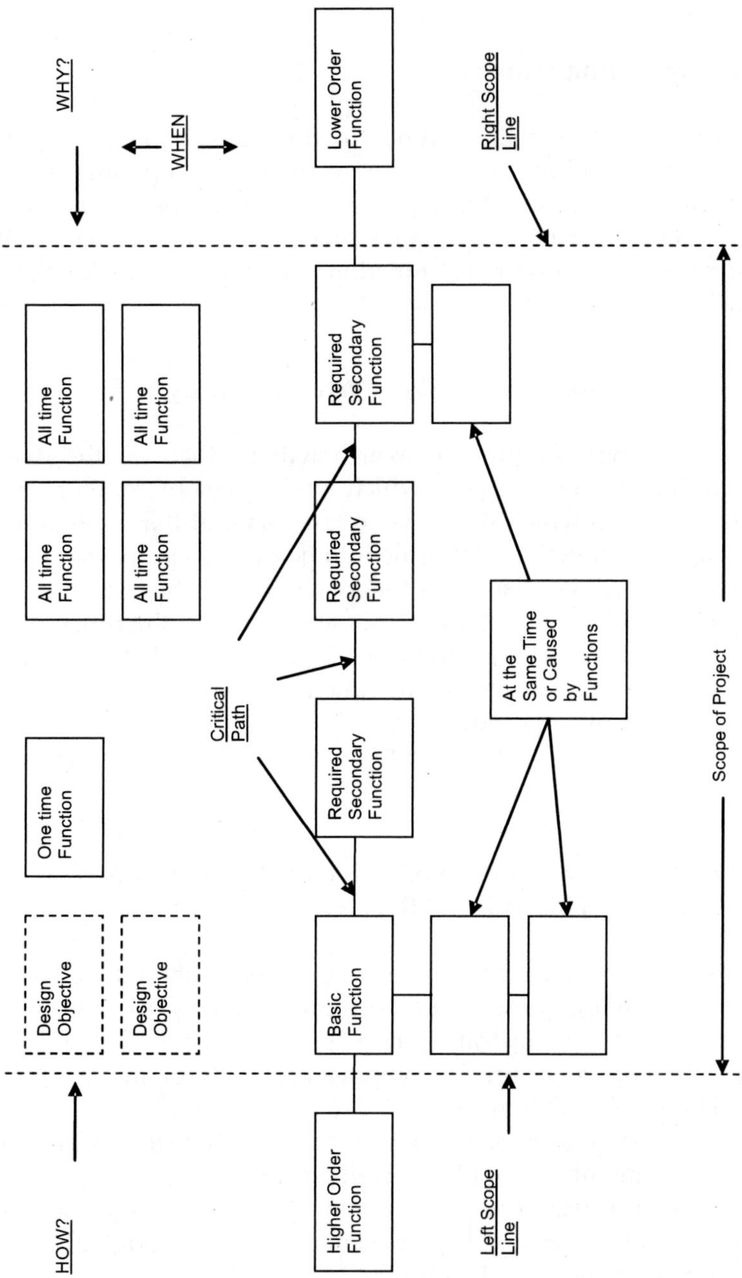

Fig. 5.1. Technically Oriented FAST Diagram.

functions are beside the design objective on the right side. There may be more than one "one-time functions". It should also be clear that not necessarily there will be one-time function at all.

5.1.10 All the Time Function

The dedicated place for these types of functions is on the right side above the critical path on the left side of the right scope line. These are those functions which are still happening when the project is not being executed. There may be many more functions of this category. Based on the above happening, these functions are known as "All the Time Functions".

5.1.11 "At the same time" and/or "Are caused by"

This is another type of function which will be there in the diagram. Any function in the critical path which when takes place, there may be some other function which will have to take place at that time. It may so happen that some function will come into being because of that function. These functions will be placed on the lower side of the critical path and will be connected by a vertical line (not arrows) with the function in the critical path. If there is more than one function which happens at the same time and/or are caused by the function, it should be placed in the descending order of importance.

These functions are called "at the same time" and/or "are caused by" functions.

5.2 HOW TO DRAW TECHNICALLY ORIENTED FAST DIAGRAM WITH ILLUSTRATION

The **first step** is to select the project. The project should be such that it is relevant, having some potential for cost saving as well as value improvement. For demonstrating how to draw the FAST diagram "a plastic jar" which is meant for keeping ear buds or swabs has been selected. The item is shown in Fig. 5.2. and Fig. 5.3.

The **second step** is to make a multi-disciplinary team. In the team at least one of the members should be well informed about the project. The author feels that at least one member should not have any background of the project. This is because his innocent and natural/original questions could lead to a breakthrough solution.

The **third step** is to find out the functions of the project, in the present case it is "a plastic jar". It is advised to use a dictionary for finding out the appropriate definition. The initial functions which have been generated are:

- Ensure quality
- Accommodate bar-code
- Produce transparency
- Withstand load
- Improve aesthetics
- Identify manufacturer
- Store material
- Display instructions
- Indicate items
- Produce shape
- Join components
- Collect components

The **fourth step** is to find out the initial basic function. The basic function is that function, if that function is not there, no other functions will exist. In Bytheways' language, **"Basic function causes all lower level functions to come into existence."**

Out of the nine functions identified, the team decided that "store material" appears to be the basic function.

Now the question is, if the function "store material" does not happen, then can the other functions *ensure quality; accommodate bar-code; produce transparency; withstand load; improve aesthetics; identify manufacturer; display*

Fig. 5.2. A Plastic Jar.

Fig. 5.3. A Plastic Jar.

instructions and indicate items exist? The answer is "no". Hence, it can be concluded that "store material" is the basic function.

The **fifth step** is to find out the higher order function. In order to find that, three basic questions are to be asked.

Qu.1 Why one has to "store material"?
Role: I am thinking as manufacturer.
A.1-1 I have to **deliver material** in good condition.
Role: I am thinking as customer.
A.1-2 I should **receive material** of proper quality.

Qu.2 What higher level function causes "store material" to come into being?
Role: I am thinking as transporter.
A.2-1 I have to **transport material** without any damage.

Qu.3 What is being accomplished when "store material" is performed?
Role: I am thinking as a store personnel.
A3-1 I need containerization to keep the product in the store. Hence, the identified function is **manufacture container**.

All the functions generated through question & answers and the initial basic functions are enumerated below:

- Deliver material
- Receive material
- Transport material
- Manufacture container
- Store material

The **sixth step** is to find the new basic function. Now, the basic function identified is "manufacture container". This has to pass through the basic function's identification test. Does "manufacture container" cause all the functions to come into being? Yes! Hence, the final basic function is "manufacture container". If one asks the question "why" to "manufacture container"? The answer will be "store material". If one asks "how" to "store material", the answer will be "manufacture container".

Hence, the higher order function will be identified as "store material".

The **seventh step** is to find out the critical path functions. Here the logic of "how" and "why" will be used. The question is "how (?)" the basic function of "manufacture container" is performed, the answer is "produce shape".

If one asks "why" to "produce shape", the answer will be to "manufacture container". Now, "how" to "produce shape", the answer will be "join components". Again "why" to "join components", the answer will be "produce shape". Hence, these two functions are fitted by the deterministic logic "how" and "why".

If one questions "how" to "join components", the answer will be "collect components". Then again if one asks "why" "collect components", the answer is "join components". Here also both the functions are fitted with the "how" and "why" logics.

The function "collect components" is not a function of the plastic jar and also a function which initiates the whole process; hence it is the lower order function.

Hence, the critical path functions are:

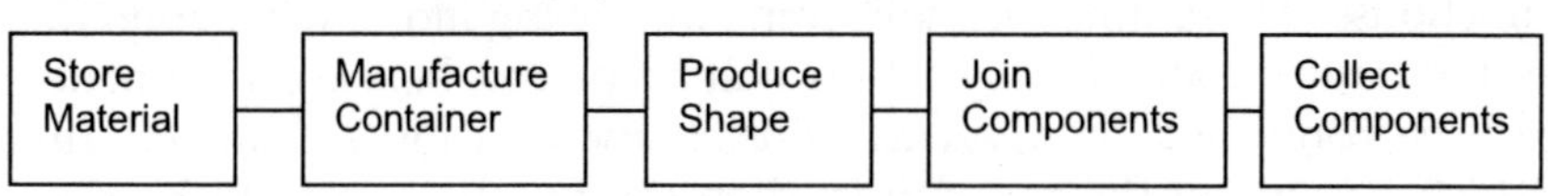

Fig. 5.4. Critical Path.

Now, the **eighth step** will be to note down all the functions so far identified. They are:

- Ensure quality
- Accommodate bar-code
- Produce transparency

- Withstand load
- Improve aesthetics
- Identify manufacturer
- Store material
- Display instructions
- Indicate items
- Transport material
- Manufacture container
- Produce shape
- Join components
- Collect components

The critical path functions are identified. Now, one has to find out the "all time functions". The "all time functions" are those functions which will always be there whether the critical functions are happening or not. Based on the above logic one can conclude the following functions as "all the time functions".

- Accommodate bar-code
- Improve aesthetics
- Identify manufacturer
- Display instructions
- Indicate items

The **ninth step** to identify "one-time function". "One-time functions" are those which will require only once of its product life. This function may be there or may not be. In this case one can identify the "one-time function" as "ensure quality".

The **tenth step** is to make the "design objectives" of the study. It is to be remembered that "design objectives" are not the functions. They are specifications; constraints or like that. In this case the "design objectives" are:

- Hold 75 stubs having 150 swabs

The **final step** will be the allocation of "at the same time or caused by functions". These functions will come into being along with some function in the critical path. This function will be placed below that function and will be connected by a vertical line. If there is more than one function which happen at the same time, then the functions should be placed in the descending order of importance. In this case, the function "produce transparency" is placed under "manufacture container" and "withstand load" under "produce shape".

When all these are completed, the dotted scope lines are to be placed in allocated places. "How"; "why" and "when" indicators are placed in their respective places. There should be an indication that what is the scope of the project.

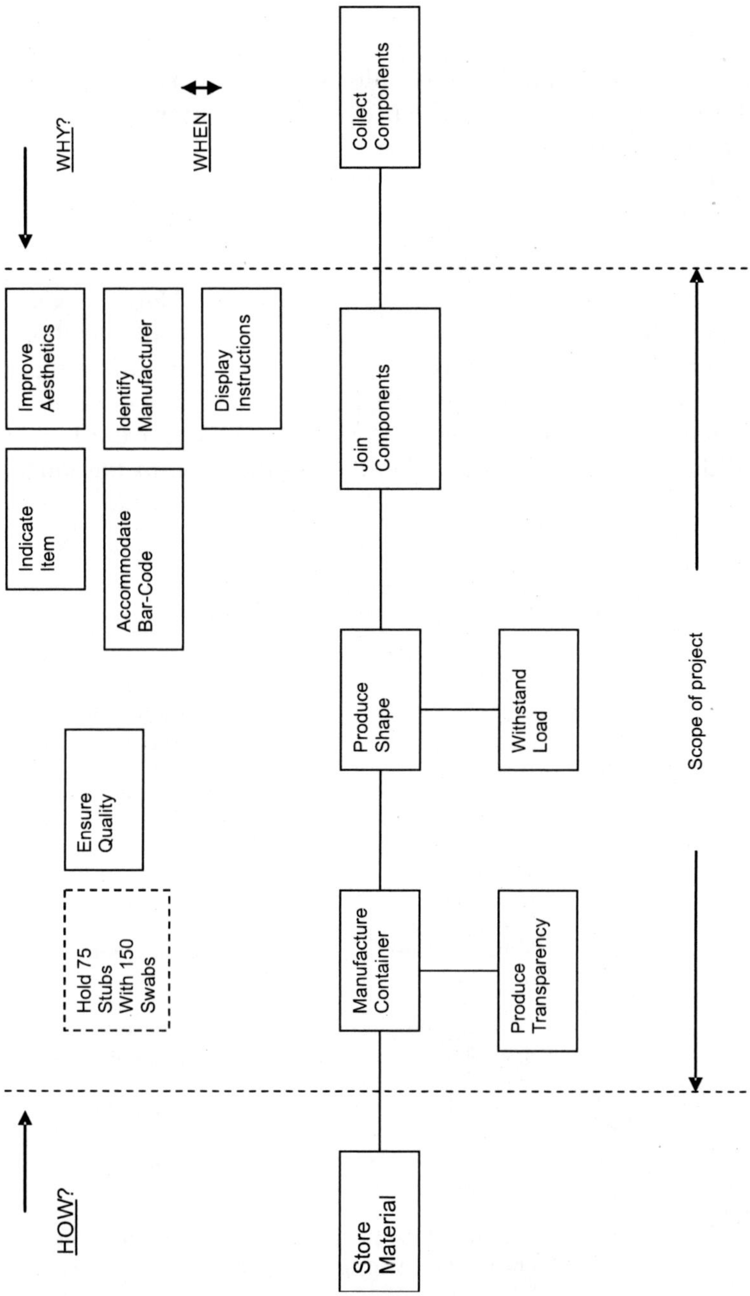

Fig. 5.5. A Plastic Jar for Ear Buds / Swabs Box (Technically Oriented FAST Diagram).

The project description has to be mentioned and also type of FAST Diagram.

5.2.1 Process

The same random identification should be done for the process also. Let us think of a simple process which everybody is doing everyday. The process may be thought of as below:

"The process of watering the garden".

Problem

Debashis Mukherjee is sitting on his porch in his New York's house, decides to water the garden. He leaves the porch, walks to the garage at the other end of the house, opens the garage door, and walks to the tool locker. There he lifts the reel of garden hose from the locker, carries it to the rear garage door, opens the door, and carries the hose to the faucet at the rear of the garage. He attaches the hose to the faucet, and begins to water the garden.

Table 5.1: Process Analysis

Travel in Ft	Symbol	Activity Description	Explanation
85	→	To garage door	He leaves the porch walks 85 ft to garage door. This is called transportation, since he moves from one place to another.
	(1)	Opens door	Opening the garage door is an operation.
10	→	To tool locker in garage	He walks 10 ft to locker to get hose. A transportation
	(2)	Removes hose from locker	This is an operation
15	→	To rear garage door	He carries hose to rear garage door. A transportation
	(3)	Opens door	This is an operation.
10	→	To faucet at rear of garage	This is transportation.
	(4)	Attaches hose to faucet and open faucet	This is considered one operation
	(5)	Waters garden	He begins the main operation of watering garden

The activity has been put in Table 5.2. To find the functions of each activity ask the question "What Does 'Activity' do?" Remember that the activity is the method of achieving the purpose, but the function is the purpose.

Table 5.2: Function Identification

Activity	Process	Function	
		Verb	**Noun**
To garage door	What does 'activity' do?	Fetch	Components
Opens door	What does 'activity' do?	Make	Way
To tool locker in garage	What does 'activity' do?	Cover	Distance
Removes hose from locker	What does 'activity' do?	Unclamp	Component
To rear garage door	What does 'activity' do?	Cover	Distance
Opens door	What does 'activity' do?	Make	Way
To faucet at rear of garage	What does 'activity' do?	Cover	Distance
Attaches hose to faucet	What does 'activity' do?	Deliver	Water
	What does 'activity' do?	Join	Components
Opens faucet	What does 'activity' do?	Allow	Water
Waters garden	What does 'activity' do?	Moisten	Soil

Draw the FAST Diagram of the process.

The Technically Oriented FAST Diagram of the process is drawn in Fig. 5.6.

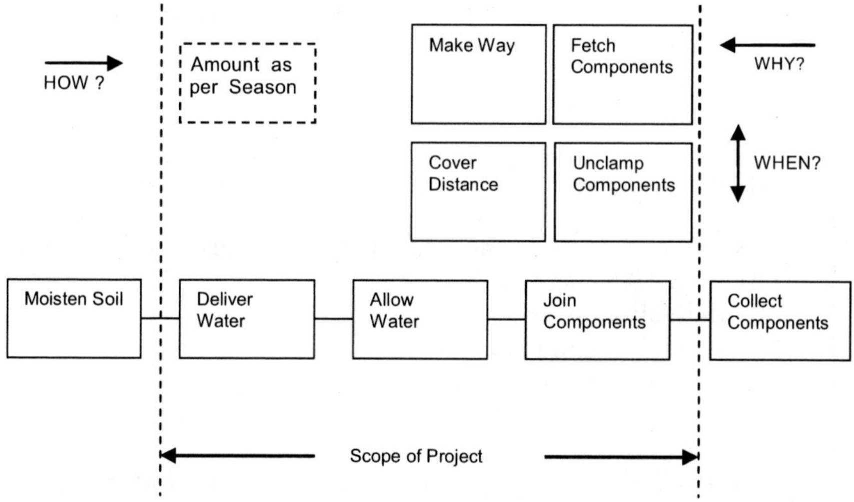

Fig. 5.6. Technically Oriented FAST Diagram.

5.3 EXERCISE

1. **Draw a format of technically oriented FAST and label it. The functions and specifications are shown in Table 5.3. Draw a technically oriented FAST diagram.**

Table 5.3:

Functions / Specifications		Functions / Specifications	
Maintain	Schedule	Train	Operators
Prepare	Material	Cast	Product
Maintain	Delivery	Minimize	Porosity
Avoid	Damage	Control	Parameter
Maintain	Equipment	Monitor	Process
Maintain	Tooling	Prepare	Material
Identify	Product	Minimize Scrap by 10%	Inspect Product after every 100
Update Equipment every month	Maintain safety at 100% level		

2. **Identify and encircle the odd function in relation to Technically Oriented FAST as per Q 1.**
   (a) Control parameter
   (b) Monitor process
   (c) Avoid damage
   (d) Follow procedures

3. **Identify and encircle the odd function in relation to Technically Oriented FAST as per Q 1.**
   (a) Maintain schedule
   (b) Maintain tooling
   (c) Minimize porosity
   (d) Identify product

4. **Identify and encircle the odd function in relation to Technically Oriented FAST as per Q 1.**
   (a) Maintain delivery
   (b) Maintain equipment
   (c) Maintain tooling
   (d) None of the above

5. **Figure 5.7 of a toothbrush is given below. Find out the functions using some systematic method and draw a Technically Oriented FAST Diagram.**

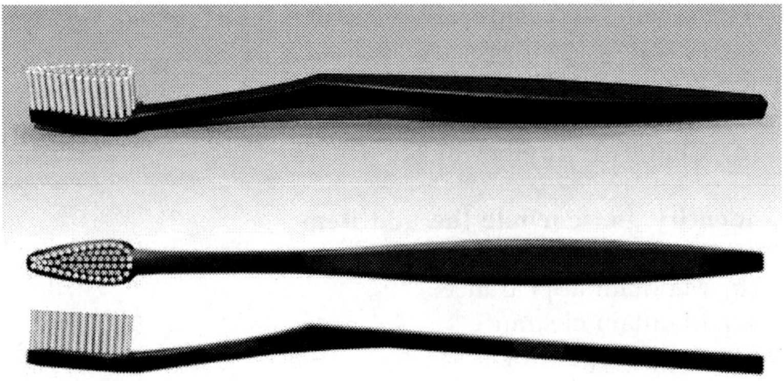

Fig. 5.7. Toothbrush.

6. **Develop a Technical FAST diagram considering the example of an overhead projection system.**
   (Innovation and Value Engineering; IEB 5; IIIE, Section B (July 2007))

7. **Develop a Technically Oriented FAST of a HB Pencil. The functions identified are shown in Table 5.4 below.**

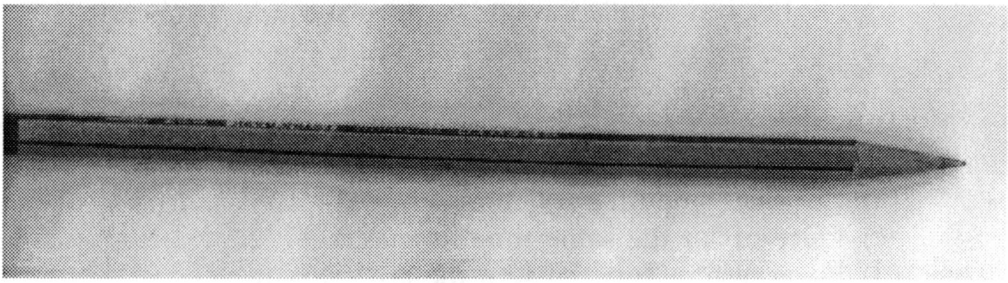

Table 5.4:

Verb	Noun	Feature
Improve	Appearance	Color
Communicate	Ideas	Requirement
Identify	Manufacturer	Print
Protect	Lead	Wood
Collect	Materials	Initiation
Indicate	Specification	Print
Make	Mark	Lead
Enable	Grip	Hexagonal
Protect	Wood	Paint
Join	Components	Glue
Ensure	Handling	Length

8. **The creator of Technically Oriented FAST is**
   (a) Arthur E. Mudge
   (b) Wayne Ruggles
   (c) T.J. Snodgrass
   (d) Charles W. Bytheway

9. **Identify and encircle the odd item**
   (a) Minimize weight by 10%
   (b) Maintain appearance
   (c) Maintain clearance
   (d) Support parking

10. **Identify and encircle the odd item**
    (a) Shelter passenger
    (b) Minimize width by 5 mm
    (c) Drain water
    (d) Ventilate tunnel

11. **Functions are not on the critical path**
    (a) Higher order function and lower order function
    (b) Basic function and one-time function
    (c) Higher order function and require secondary function
    (d) Lower order function and basic function

12. **In which place "how" and "why" logic is applicable to**
    (a) Place of "design objectives"
    (b) Place of "one-time functions"
    (c) Place of "at the same time function"
    (d) Place of the "functions on the critical path"

13. **Identify the item which was not available in the basic FAST model**
    (a) Critical path
    (b) One-time function
    (c) Higher order function
    (d) Basic function

14. **Make a comparison between Basic FAST Model and Technically Oriented FAST Model.**

15. **What is the relationship between G and B? Refer to Fig. 5.8.**
    (a) Both are basic functions
    (b) Both are one time functions
    (c) Both are all the time functions
    (d) None of the above

16. Find out the basic function in Fig. 5.8

(a) Function L (b) Function I
(c) Function F (d) Function J

17. What is the relationship among M, L, C in Fig. 5.8?

(a) One-time functions
(b) All the time functions
(c) Basic and required secondary functions
(d) Required secondary functions

18. What is the relationship among K, H, F in Fig. 5.8?

(a) At the same time function
(b) One-time function
(c) All the time function
(d) All unnecessary functions

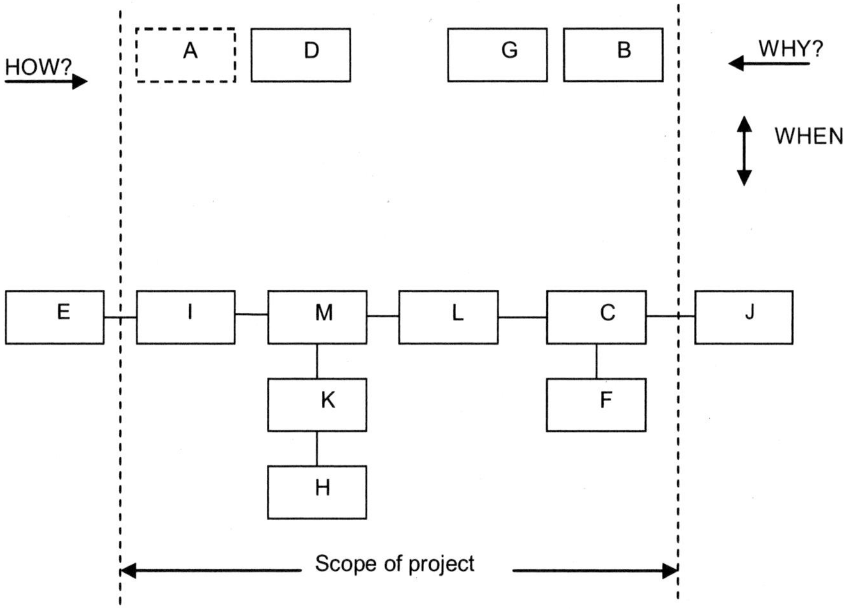

Fig. 5.8. Technically Oriented FAST.

19. Function M in comparison to function L, in Fig. 5.8 is

(a) Same function (b) Higher order function
(c) Lower order function (d) Basic function

20. Find out the design objective in Fig. 5.8

(a) E (b) J
(c) A (d) D

21. Find out the "one-time function" in Fig. 5.8

(a) D (b) L
(c) A (d) J

22. What is the name of function J in Fig. 5.8?

(a) Required secondary function
(b) Causative function
(c) At the same time function
(d) One-time function

23. Identify the highest order function in Fig. 5.8

(a) D (b) M
(c) I (d) E

CHAPTER

6

Customer-Oriented FAST

"The Customer-Oriented FAST emphasizes the fact that success cannot be achieved unless users' / owners' needs and desires are recognized, understood and fulfilled."

– Thomas J. Snodgrass and Muthiah Kasi

6.1 INTRODUCTION

The development of Customer-Oriented FAST Diagramming is the subsequent development after the Technically Oriented FAST Diagramming. The marketing and sales personnel felt that to sell the product, Technically Oriented FAST is not an appropriate tool to convince the customers. Other than the use functions there are a lot of functions which require convincing the customers. This need was felt by T. S. Snodgrass and Ted Fowler and they developed this concept of Customer-Oriented FAST Diagramming.

The Customer-Oriented FAST Diagramming is basically a holistic approach towards the total product, process or system. Here in this technique the deterministic logics like "how" and "why" are used. The nomenclature is different as per the new techniques.

6.2 COMPARATIVE ANALYSIS OF EXPERTS' OPINIONS

There were distinct differences in viewpoints of Miles, Bytheway and Snodgrass. Table 6.1 elaborates this.

Table 6.1: Comparative Analysis of Experts' Opinions

Miles	Bytheway	Snodgrass
--	--	Task
Function Specifications	Design Objectives	--
Use Function	Use Value	Basic Functions
Aesthetic Functions	Aesthetic or Unwanted	Primary Supporting Functions
Basic Functions	Basic Functions	Primary Basic Functions
*Required	*Required Secondary Functions	*Secondary Basic Functions
*2nd Degree or Secondary	*All-the-Time Functions *At-the-Same-Time functions	Or *Primary or Secondary Supporting Functions
Functions	Critical path	--
--	Scope	--
	Philosophy	
"Only Basic Function Contributes to Value"	"Only Basic Function Contributes to Value"	"All Functions Contribute to Value"

(Source: *"The User-Oriented FAST Diagram"* by Theodre C. Fowler, CVS, The Freelance Group, Inc, Fairborn, Ohio, Vol. 18; pp. 89-94.)

6.3 PREREQUISITES

In this technique some actions are to be done before starting to draw the FAST diagram. These are important to achieve a meaningful result. These are discussed below.

6.3.1 Team

The first requirement is a multidisciplinary team. In this technique one member of the team should thoroughly know about the project. That member should be considered the key resource.

6.3.2 Cost Data

The cost data is an important aspect of the value engineering study. Here, in this technique detailed cost data is essential because customers correlate cost with the value.

6.3.3 Users' Attitude

This aspect is new to this technique. The users are to be kept in mind while drawing the Customer-Oriented FAST Diagram. It is important to have detailed information of the customers' attitudes. It is better to have a survey of customers or have the preferences of the customers through market research agencies, if available. This will help to identify the key requirements and will try to incorporate them in the project. It is always advisable that it should be readily available during the course of the study.

In this connection, Thomas J. Snodgrass and Muthiah Kasi's views expressed in their book "*Function Analysis: The Stepping Stones to Good Value*" are relevant. They say, "There is vast difference between wanted and needed functions. Sometimes these two terms are not distinctly differentiated. This results in waste of resources. When an owner/user wants a function, the owner may think the function is needed. In a VE study, wanted functions are brought to the attention of the owner/user. If the owner/user still wants them, they can be provided. In most cases, wanted functions which cost less will be included, wanted functions that cost more will be excluded. In all cases, the decision should be made by the owner, not the designer."

Though this case pertains to the construction industry, it is useful for other application areas too.

6.3.4 Key Resource Provides Formal Description

The key team member should appraise all the members in detail about the project. If required the group should go to the project site and gain clarity about the project, in terms of the method of manufacturing, method of transportation or any other details which may need to be observed. The key person is supposed to explain the details of manufacturing and/or the problems encountered.

6.4 SALIENT FEATURES

There are certain features of this FAST diagramming which are different from what has been enumerated in earlier sections. These salient features are enumerated below.

6.4.1 Task

The **task** is similar to higher order function of both Classical FAST and Technically Oriented FAST. This is the objective or goal or the requirement of the management. This is a function and should be of two words—an active verb and a measurable noun. The scope line will be placed on the right side of this block.

6.4.2 Scope Line

In this type of FAST diagramming there is only one scope line and that is on the right side of the task. This line should be a dotted line. The scope of the project starts after this scope line. There is no right scope line as in other FAST diagrams.

6.4.3 "How-Why" Logic

The deterministic logic like "how-why" is also used in this technique. The "how" logic will be from the left side to the right side, whereas "why" logic will be from the right side to the left side. The answer of "how" will be the lower order function and the answer of "why" will be the higher order function. In order to accept any function both the "how" and "why" logics should be satisfied. Here, in this technique all functions are connected with "how" and "why" logics.

6.4.4 Levels

If one draws imaginary vertical lines after the scope line, then each imaginary vertical line will represent a level. The first imaginary vertical line which is on the right side of the scope line is called the first level. Then the second imaginary line will be the second level and so on. The functions which will be placed on the first vertical line are called first level of functions. Similarly, there will be second and third levels of functions and so on. One can go from one level to the next lower level by asking "how" question.

6.4.5 Basic Functions

The primary functions are placed on the top half of the FAST diagram. There are various levels of primary functions. They are mentioned as below.

6.4.5.1 Primary Basic Function

The primary basic function is the function for which the value engineering project has been created. This is placed in the top portion of the diagram and should be a block of solid lines. It is called the first level of function. There may be more than one first level of primary basic function. These primary basic functional blocks are placed on the first imaginary vertical line after the scope line. If "how" is asked for the "task", the answer should be primary basic function. Similarly, if the question "why" is asked for the primary basic function the answer should be the "task". If it is not satisfied, the team should redefine or find out a different function which can satisfy both the logics.

6.4.5.2 *Secondary Basic Function*

If one asks "how" for the primary basic function, one may get function or functions which will be the second level of primary basic function.

6.4.6 Supporting Function

This is the unique part of this particular FAST diagramming technique. It has been mentioned earlier that the whole concept comes into being keeping in mind the customers' acceptance and users' needs. Based on this assumption the first level of supporting functions have already been identified and fixed. These have been enumerated in detail below. The second level of supporting function will be generated by asking the "how" questions.

6.4.6.1 *Assure Convenience*

The first functional need identified for customers and users is "assure convenience". The product will be sold if this aspect is available with the product/process/system. This will force the team to identify the functions which will provide this first level function. For the benefit of the readers Table 6.2 is provided.

Table 6.2: Functions in "Assure Convenience"

Verb	Noun	Verb	Noun
Facilitate	Installation	Instruct	Users
Instruct	Customers	Facilitate	Service
Facilitate	Maintenance	Indicate	Availability

6.4.6.2 *Assure Dependability*

Customers and users should feel that the product/process/system they purchase is dependable. If in the formation of Customer-Oriented FAST Diagramming, team members identify those functions, it becomes easy to convince the customers and users. This will, in turn, increase the sale of the product/process/system. Table 6.3 indicates those types of functions.

Table 6.3: Functions in "Assure Dependability"

Verb	Noun	Verb	Noun
Facilitate	Shipment	Protect	Serviceman
Resist	Deterioration	Eliminate	Theft
Protect	Customer	Protect	Surroundings

6.4.6.3 *Satisfy Customer*

Customer satisfaction is the goal of any product. This is because one has to incorporate certain features in the product/process/system. The "how" question to "satisfy customer" generates various lower level functions. These functions will help to market the product/process/system. The following functions shown in Table 6.4 will help the readers.

Table 6.4: Functions in "Satisfy Customer"

Verb	Noun	Verb	Noun
Fit	Surroundings	Minimize	Part-Inventory
Ensure	Adjustment	Ensure	Optimum-Capacity
Minimize	Selections	Optimize	Quality
Minimize	Noise	Minimize	Service
Adequate	Instructions	Pictorial	Instructions

6.4.6.4 *Attract Customer*

If the product does not attract a customer, there will be lower sale of the product/process/system. For marketing and sale of the product/process/system this feature is very important. This sale function will differentiate between two products/processes/systems. The action starts from viewing the product/process/system. The following examples shown in Table 6.5 will help the readers.

Table 6.5: Items to "Attract Customer"

Items	Items	Items	Items
Style (Product)	Color	Weight	Round Shape
Color Combination	Square Shape	Rectangular Shape	Packaging
Space	Speed	Style (Statement)	Smell
Printing	Engraving		

6.5 RULES OF DRAWING FAST

Before embarking on drawing a Customer-Oriented FAST Diagram, it is worthwhile to know the rules of drawing the FAST diagram. The rules are enumerated as below:

1. Scope line to be a dotted line.
2. There is only one on the left hand side scope line.
3. "How" to be mentioned on left side of the scope line.
4. Primary functions will be on the top.
5. There should be a mention of "support functions" under the "primary function".
6. Accepted first level supporting functions should be mentioned.
7. While branching, there should be at least two or more branching.
8. Name of the project should be mentioned either on the top or on the bottom.

6.6 HOW TO DRAW FAST DIAGRAM

A. The team should choose a systematic method to identify the functions. The team can follow the following rules to garner the maximum advantage. They are,
   1. Always use just two words which include an active verb first, followed by a measurable noun.
   2. Verbs such as 'provide' is generally not considered 'active' verbs.
   3. Measurable nouns should be just those nouns that can be measured.
   4. Specific component or process names should not be used if possible.
   5. Function should be as general as possible and yet still describe the process to be evaluated.
   6. Similar functions should be allowed to be generated as long as either the verb or noun is different from those previously mentioned.
   7. All aspects of the manufacturing process should be considered both from the customer's perspective as well as from the manufacturer's perspective.
   8. Extensive use of dictionary during the process of identifying and defining functions.

B. Make a list of functions generated and write them in a "Fit-it™" small pad. This promotes visibility for the team when they set out to make the FAST diagram.

C. Out of the functions generated, find out what may be best suited for primary basic function(s).
D. Ask "why" question to this new primary basic function(s). The answer will be "task".
E. To validate the "task" ask "how" for the task. If the answer is the same as the primary basic function(s), then the relationship is established. If not, find out a different function which will satisfy both the deterministic logics.
F. Now ask the "how" question for the primary basic function and find out which functions satisfy that question. The Rule No. A-7 should be followed.
G. If one finds only one function during branching, the team should go into more details about that. This aspect is brought out clearly in an article, The "User Oriented" FAST Diagram by Theodore C. Fowler, 1983 SAVE Conference Proceedings Vol. 18; pp. 89-94, which mentions - "The rationale for this seemingly arbitrary rule: "If one function is followed by another single function, the second one is simply a redefinition of the first at a LOWER LEVEL OF ABSTRACTION."
H. All functions should be validated by "how" and "why" logics.
I. When the primary function line is complete then one should proceed to the supporting functions.
J. Since the first level of supporting function is already established, isolate functions which had been generated earlier in the different categories like "assure convenience", "assure dependability", "satisfy customer" and "attract customer".
K. Start with "assure convenience". Ask question "how" for the "assure convenience" and find out the function from among the functions identified. The Rule No. A-7 should be kept in mind.
L. Ask question "why" for all the functions and check whether one gets "assure convenience" as the answer. If the answers are validated, then the placement of functions is correct. These validated functions will then be the second level of functions for the supporting function, "assure convenience".
M. The procedure will be followed for the third level and onwards.
N. The same procedure from K-M should be followed for other supporting functions.

The format for Customer Oriented FAST is shown in Fig. 6.1.

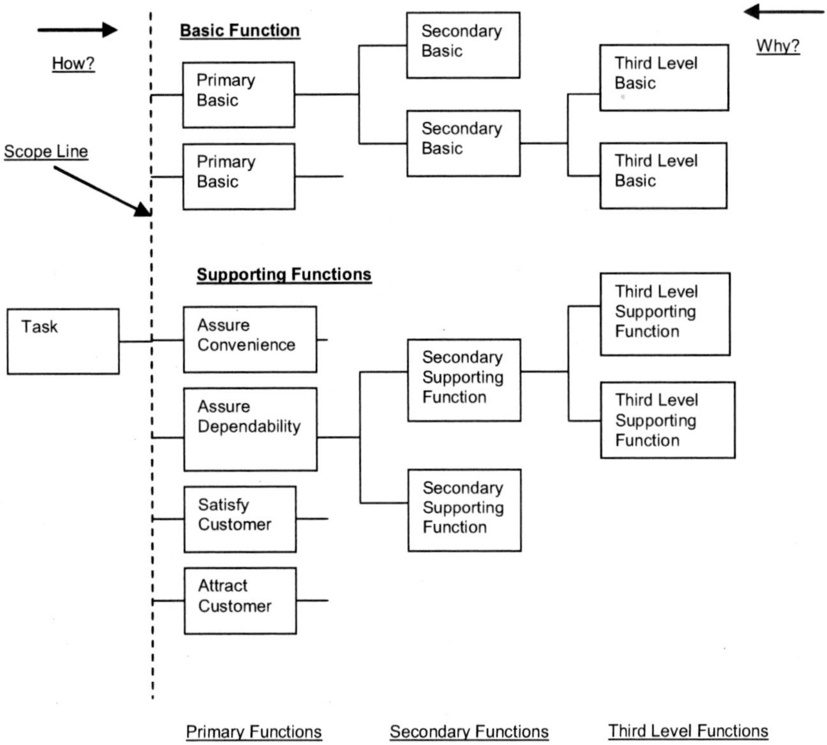

Fig. 6.1. Customer-Oriented FAST Diagram.

6.7 ILLUSTRATION

6.7.1 Product

As an example, a screwdriver, shown in Fig. 6.2, has been chosen for an easy illustration. The functions of a screwdriver are given in Table 6.6. The Customer-Oriented FAST Diagram will be as in Fig. 6.2.

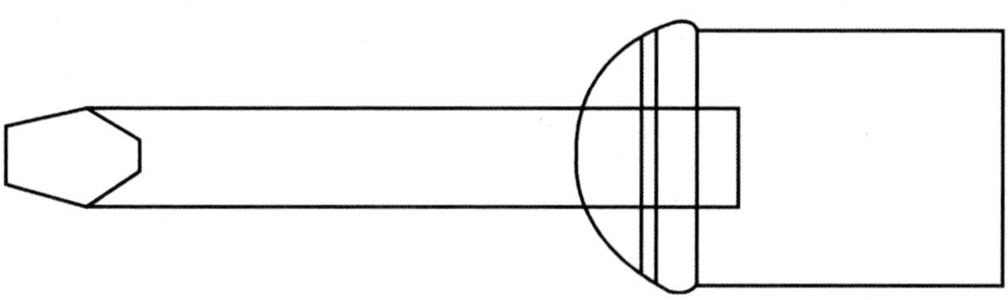

Fig. 6.2. Screwdriver.

Table 6.6: Functions of a Screwdriver

Verb	Noun	Verb	Noun
Receive	Torque	Transmit	Torque
Ensure	Approach	Allow	Pin
Prevent	Crack	Prevent	Rust
Join	Components	Prevent	Wood
Withstand	Torque	Suit	Slot

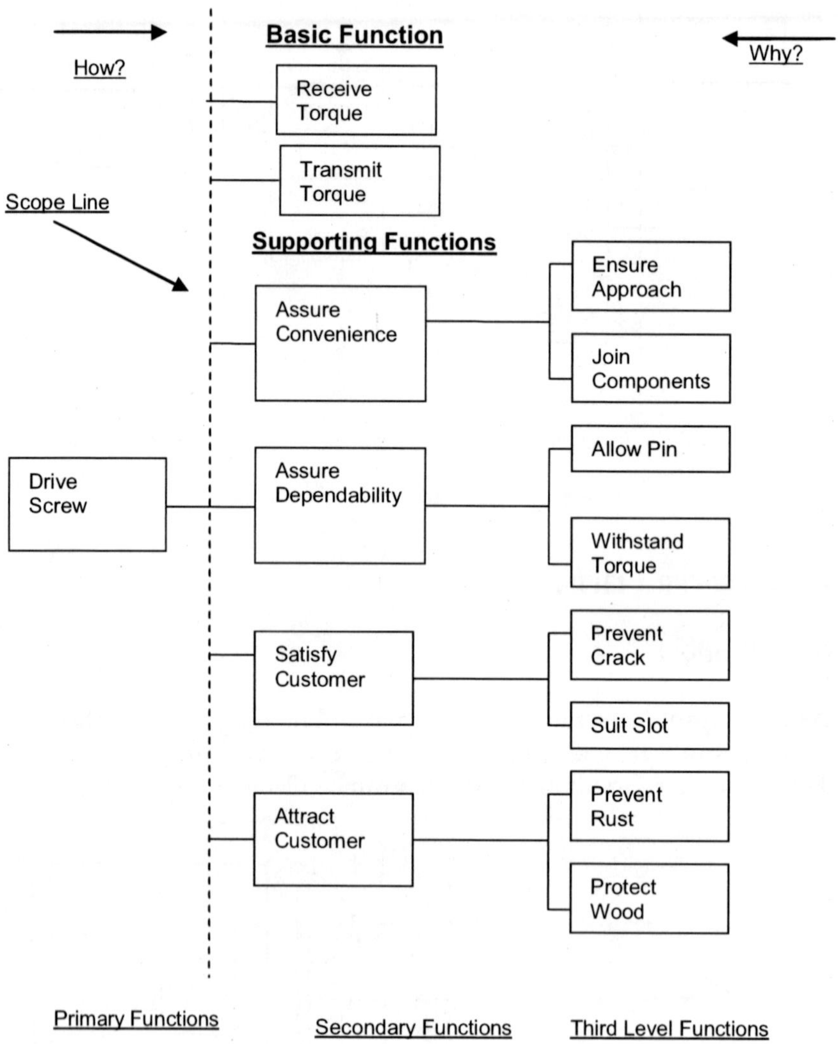

Fig. 6.3. Customer-Oriented FAST Diagram of a Screwdriver.

6.7.2 System

6.7.2.1 *Software Development Life Cycle*

Software testing is the sub-system of software development life cycle (SDLC). When a developer finishes the design or coding of an application, it needs to be thoroughly scrutinized for any bugs that might have crept in owing to faulty design or code, which is called testing.

There are two types of testing; one which is done by the developer himself and the other done by a professional tester. The professional tester checks the software from the users' perspective. The tester has to follow certain procedures. The following is an indicative daily schedule of a principal software testing engineer.

9 – 9:30 am: Check e-mail, look for customer feedback on the last release.

9:30 – 10 am: Team meeting (with developers, testers and managers) to discuss the feedback and problems reported, collect information on the problem (that is, the kind of operating software, browser, JavaScript version at the customer end and so on).

10 – 1 pm: Prepare a strategy to investigate the issue and analyze the tests needed, brainstorm with teammates on strategy.

1 – 2 pm: Lunch break, discuss alternative solution.

2 – 4 pm: At workstation, figuring out if the solution works, and if the situations are reproducible in the last environment.

4 – 6 pm: Test the best solution under various conditions; prepare a report identifying the root cause of the problem.

6 – 7 pm: Gather evidence to support her/his report.

Table 6.7: Activity Function Matrix

Time	Activity	Question	Function
9–9:30 am	1. Check e-mail 2. Look for customer on the last release	What does it do?	1. Examine Mail 2. Receive Customer - Feedback
9:30–10 am	1. Team meeting (with developers, testers and managers) to discuss the feedback and problems reported 2. Collect information on the problem (that is, the kind of operating software, browser, JavaScript version at the customer end and so on)	What does it do?	1. Discuss Problem 2. Collect Information
10–1 pm	1. Prepare a strategy to investigate the issue	What does it do?	1. Develop Strategy

Contd.

Table 6.7: Contd.

	2. Brainstorm with teammates on strategy		2. Create Ideas
1–2 pm	1. Discussion alternative solution during lunch	What does it do?	1. Discuss Probable Solution
2–4 pm	1. At workstation, figuring out if the solution will work, 2. If the situations are reproducible in last environment	What does it do?	1. Test Probable Solution
4–6 pm	1. Test the best solution under various conditions 2. Prepare a report identifying the root cause of the problem	What does it do?	1. Arrive at Solution 2. Identify Root Cause 3. Prepare Report
6–7 pm	1. Gather evidence to support her/his report 2. Draft e-mail for the customer 3. Answer other e-mail	What does it do?	1. Document Evidence 2. Draft Mail 3. Reply Mail

The Customer-Oriented FAST Diagram is drawn as shown in Fig. 6.4.

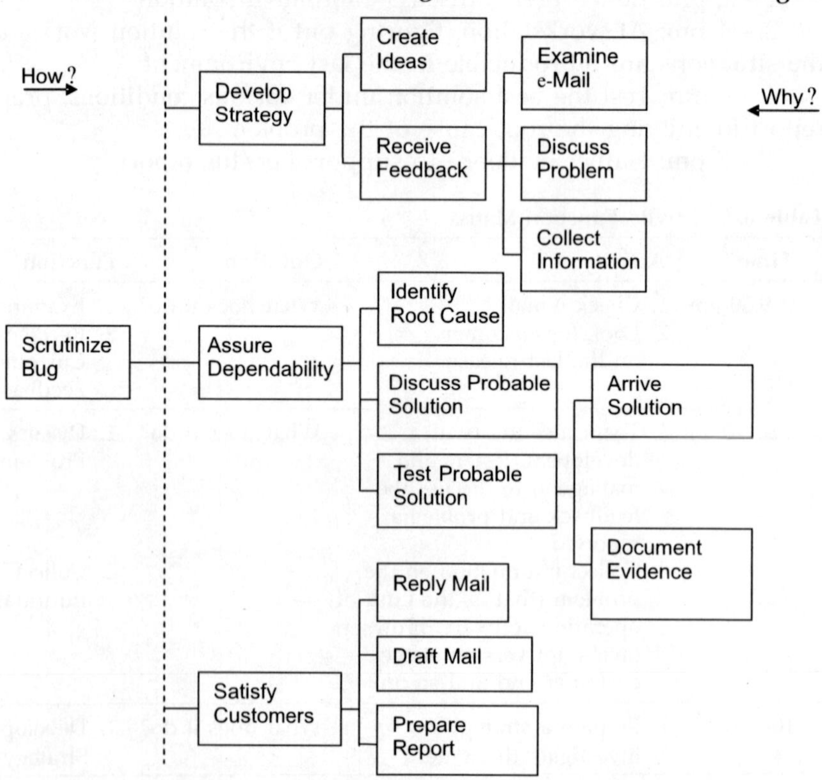

Fig. 6.4. Customer Oriented FAST Diagram of Software Testing System.

6.8 EXERCISE

1. **Distinguish between Customer-Oriented FAST diagram and Technical Oriented FAST diagram.**
   (*IEB 5 Innovation and Value Engineering, IIIE, Section B; January 2007*)

2. **Develop a Customer-Oriented FAST of a pencil. The functions identified in Table 6.8 are as below.**

Table 6.8:

Verb	Noun	Feature
Improve	Appearance	Color
Communicate	Ideas	Requirement
Identify	Manufacturer	Print
Protect	Lead	Wood
Collect	Materials	Initiation
Indicate	Specification	Print
Make	Mark	Lead
Enable	Grip	Hexagonal
Protect	Wood	Paint
Join	Components	Glue
Ensure	Handling	Length

3. **The creator of Customer-Oriented FAST is**
   (a) L.D. Miles and Arthur E. Mudge
   (b) Wayne Ruggles and R.J. Park
   (c) T.J. Snodgrass and Theodore Fowler
   (d) Charles W. Bytheway and Cyril Tammadge

4. **Identify and encircle the odd item.**
   (a) Facilitate shipment (b) Protect customer
   (c) Facilitate installation (d) Protect surroundings

5. **Identify and encircle the odd items**

   (a) Instruct user (b) Improve appearance

   (c) Facilitate service (d) Indicate availability

6. **Write short notes on supporting functions of the Customer-Oriented FAST Diagram. Mention at least three functions in each supporting functions.**

7. **Identify and encircle the odd one.**

   (a) Optimize quality (b) Receive torque

   (c) Minimize service (d) Pictorial instructions

8. **The higher order function in Customer-Oriented FAST is**

   (a) Objective (b) Target

   (c) Task (d) Goal

9. **Which is not a supporting function in Customer-Oriented FAST?**

   (a) Assure convenience (b) Satisfy customer

   (c) Attract customer (d) Assure comfort ability

10. **The place of primary functions are in the**

    (a) Middle (b) Top

    (c) Bottom (d) Any place decided by team

11. **The minimum branching from one function should be**

    (a) 4 (b) 3

    (c) 2 (d) 1

12. **Which one of the following is a prerequisite of Customer-Oriented FAST**

    (a) Users' attitude

    (b) Management's behavior

    (c) Environment of the organization

    (d) Type of the organization

13. **The philosophy of Customer-Oriented FAST, as envisaged by Snodgrass is**

    (a) Only basic function contributes to value

    (b) Only secondary functions contribute to value

    (c) All functions contribute to value

    (d) Not sure which function will contribute to value

14. "How" and "why" logics are applicable to
(a) Only in basic functions
(b) All basic and supporting functions
(c) Only in supporting functions
(d) Functions to be decided by the team

15. In the Customer-Oriented FAST, the scope line will be
(a) On the right side of the diagram
(b) On both right and left side of the diagram
(c) On the left side of the diagram
(d) On the discretion of the team leader

16. The imaginary vertical line which is on the right side of the scope line is called
(a) Centre level (b) First level
(c) Second level (d) Third level

17. Point out the first level of supporting function
(a) Satisfy management (b) Satisfy union
(c) Satisfy customer (d) Satisfy employee

18. The first level functions is also known as
(a) Primary function
(b) Secondary function
(c) Required secondary function
(d) Important function

19. Match the following functions shown in Table 6.9.

Table 6.9:

a	Satisfy customer	A	Facilitate installation
b	Assure dependability	B	Prevent rust
c	Attract customer	C	Eliminate theft
d	Assure convenience	D	Minimize noise

20. Match the following functions shown in Table 6.10.

Table 6.10:

a	Assure convenience	A	Protect serviceman
b	Assure dependability	B	Minimize part-inventory
c	Satisfy customer	C	Pick-up speed
d	Attract customer	D	Instruct users

21. What are the different types of FAST? Write about one FAST diagram and its construction.

CHAPTER

7

Function Cost Allocation

"All cost is for function." – *Lawrence D. Miles*

7.1 COST ALLOCATION

In value engineering methodology the product cost has to be converted into functional cost. Because of this, the method of allocation of product cost to functional cost has become so important. The advantage of this allocation is that if the function could be eliminated the cost will also get eliminated.

If a part of the product has a single function, then there is no problem of allocating the cost to the function. The problem will start when there are many functions of the same part. In that case, one has to devise some methodology to allocate the cost to different functions. There are certain basic rules which should be followed to find out the cost of functions. The procedure for allocation of cost are enumerated below.

7.1.1 Procedure for Cost Allocation

1. Split the product into components and service/system into activities.
2. Define functions of components/activities.
3. Divide total cost of product/service/system into components/activities cost.
4. Process performed to achieve particular function—cost allocated to that function.

5. Component provided to achieve particular function—cost allocated to that function.
6. Component accomplishes more than one function—allocation should be based on certain technical considerations like weight, volume, surface area, and length. Alternately, the team can come up with some innovative ideas too.

7.1.2 Basic Rules

1. Hold each function in isolation.
2. Select one function first.
3. Find out a comparable item that does not have the other two functions.
4. Determine the cost of that item. This cost will be the function cost of the first function.
5. Then, select the second function.
6. Find out another comparable item where the first and second functions are there.
7. Determine the cost of that item.
8. The difference between (7) and (4) will indicate the functional cost of the second function.
9. The above procedure will help to find out the functional cost of the third and other functions, if any.

7.1.3 Illustration

In order to illustrate the method of finding out the function cost, a known item has been taken. It is a screwdriver. The screwdriver has two components, one is the blade made of steel and the other is the handle. The cost of the screwdriver is Rs. 13.46. The blade costs Rs. 7.36 and the handle made of plastic costs Rs. 6.10. The blade has a number functions such as:

1. Suit slot
2. Ensure approach
3. Transmit torque
4. Withstand torque
5. Prevent rusting
6. Join components

The screwdriver is shown in Fig. 7.1 below.

In order to allocate the cost of the blade to all six functions Table 7.1 may be of help.

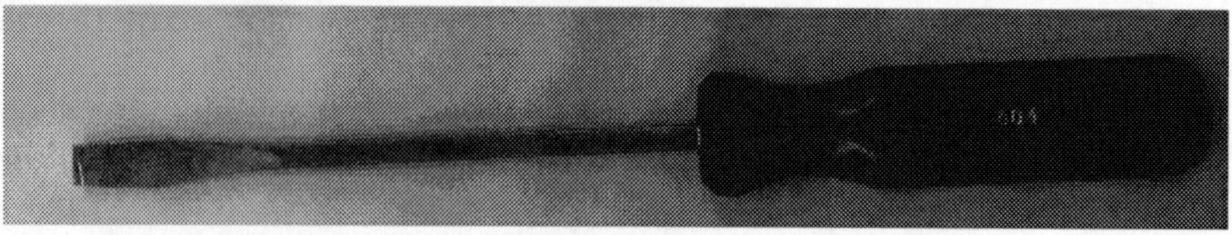

Fig. 7.1. Screwdriver.

Table 7.1: Technical Considerations for Allocating Cost (Blade)

Function		Material Cost	Labor Cost of				Overhead
Verb	**Noun**		**Manu-facturing**	**Forging**	**Heat treatment**	**Chromium Plating**	
Suit	Slot			yes			yes
Ensure	Approach	4 mm dia. × (L-l)	Machi--ning				yes
Transmit	Torque	(10-4) mm dia × (L-l)					
Withstand	Torque				yes		yes
Prevent	Rusting					yes	yes
Join	Compo-nents	10 mm dia × l					

Legend:
1. "L" is the total length of the blade.
2. "l" is the length inside the handle.
3. "4 mm dia" and length (L-l) is sufficient to approach
4. Extra "6 mm dia" and length (L-l) is sufficient to transmit torque.

Similarly, the functions of handle can be enumerated as below:

1. Receive torque
2. Join components
3. Withstand torque
4. Facilitate grip
5. Improve aesthetics

Table 7.2 enumerates the technical considerations for allocating cost to different functions of the handle.

Table 7.2: Technical Considerations for Allocating Cost (Handle)

Function		**Material Cost**	**Labor Cost of**				**Overhead**
Verb	**Noun**		**Manu-facturing**	**Forging**	**Heat treatment**	**Chromium Plating**	
Receive	Torque	Cost of low grade plastic					
Join	Compo-nents		Molding				yes
Withstand	Torque	Cost difference of high and low grade plastic					
Facilitate	Grip		Outer Shape				yes
Improve	Aesthe-tics	Material difference between color and without color					

7.1.3.1 Cost Calculation of Screwdriver

The technical details of the screwdriver are:

Blade

(1) Length (L_1) 12.50 cm
(2) Diameter (d_1) 1.00 cm
(3) Length inside the handle (l_1) 2.5 cm
(4) Diameter (d_2) 0.40 cm
(5) Material cost Rs. 25.00 per kg
(6) Steel density 0.008 kg/cc
(7) Manufactured 100 pcs per hr. Labour Cost = Rs. 50.00 per hr. Overhead 100% of labour cost
(8) Forging 125 pcs per hr. Labour Cost = Rs. 75.00 per hr. Overhead 125% of labour cost
(9) Heat treatment 125 pcs per hr. Labour Cost = Rs.75.00 per hr. Overhead cost 200% of labour cost
(10) Plating 100 pcs per hr. Labour cost = Rs. 50.00 per hr. Overhead cost 150% of labour cost.

Handle

(1) Length of handle (L_2) 7.5 cm
(2) Diameter of handle (d_2) 2.5 cm
(3) Material cost (Polypropylene - without color) Rs. 110 per kg.
(4) Material cost (Polypropylene - with color) Rs. 115 per kg.
(5) Density 0.00085 kg/cc
(6) Moulding 150 pcs per hour. Labour cost = Rs. 75 per hr; Overhead = 200% of labour cost
(7) Material cost (Low quality) Rs. 50 per kg
(8) Die manufacturing cost = Rs. 1,00,000 per die (outsource), which produces 1,00,000 components.

COST CALCULATION

Cost Calculation of Blade

Material cost

Material cost of blade (1 cm dia × 12.5 cm length)
= $3.14/4 \times 1^2 \times 12.5 \times 0.008 \times 25$ = Rs. 1.962
Material cost of Blade (0.4 cm dia × 12.5 cm length)
= $3.14/4 \times 0.4^2 \times 12.5 \times 0.008 \times 25$ = Re. 0.314
Material cost of 10.00 cm length by 0.4 cm dia.
= $0.314/12.5 \times 10$ = Re. 0.251
Material cost of 10.00 cm length by 1.0 cm dia
= $1.962/12.5 \times 10$ = Rs. 1.570
Material cost of 2.50 cm length by 1.0 cm dia
= (1.962 - 1.570) = Re. 0.392

Labor cost

Labor cost of manufacturing = $1/100 \times$ Rs. 50 = Re. 0.50
Labor cost of forging = $1/125 \times$ Rs. 75 = Re. 0.60
Labor cost of heat treatment = $1/1.25 \times$ Rs. 75 = Re. 0.60
Labor cost of plating = $1/100 \times$ Rs. 50 = Re. 0.50

Overhead cost

Overhead cost of manufacturing = 0.50×1.00 = Re. 0.50
Overhead cost of forging = 0.60×1.25 = Re. 0.75
Overhead cost of heat treatment = 0.60×2.00 = Rs. 1.20
Overhead cost of plating = $0.50 \times 1.5 = 0.75$

Table 7.3: Function Cost Allocation (Blade)

Function		**Material Cost**	**Labor Cost of**				**Over-head**	**Total Cost**
Verb	**Noun**		**Manu-facturing**	**Forging**	**Heat treatment**	**Chromium Plating**		
Suit	Slot			0.60			0.75	1.35
Ensure	Appro-ach	0.25	0.50				0.50	1.25
Transmit	Torque	1.32						1.32
Withstand	Torque				0.60		1.20	1.80
Prevent	Rusting					0.50	0.75	1.25
Join	Compo-nents	0.39						0.39
							Total	7.36

Cost Calculation of Handle

Material cost

Material cost of polystyrene material (without color)
$= 3.14/4 \times 2.5^2 \times 7.5 \times 0.00085 \times 110 =$ Rs. 3.44
Material cost of polystyrene material (with color)
$= 3.14/4 \times 2.5^2 \times 7.5 \times 0.00085 \times 115 =$ Rs. 3.60
Material cost of low quality plastic
$= 3.44/110 \times 50 =$ Rs. 1.56

Labour cost

Labor cost of molding $= 1/150 \times 75 =$ Re. 0.50;
Overhead cost $= 2.00 \times 0.5 =$ Re. 1.00
Cost of shaping = Die manufacturing cost/No. of products per die
= 1,00,000 / 1,00,000 = Re. 1.00.

Table 7.4: Function Cost Allocation (Handle)

Function		**Material Cost**	**Labor Cost of**				**Over-head**	**Total Cost**
Verb	**Noun**		**Manu-facturing**	**Forging**	**Heat treatment**	**Chromium Plating**		
Receive	Torque	1.56						1.56
Join	Compo-nents		0.50				1.00	1.50
Withstand	Torque	1.88						1.88
Facilitate	Grip		1.00					1.00
Improve	Aesthe-tics	0.16						0.16
							Total	6.10

7.1.4 Summary of Functions and Functions Costs

The functions and the functions costs are summarized in Table 7.5.

Table 7.5: Summary of Functions and Functions Costs

Functions		Function Cost
Verb	**Noun**	
Suit	Slot	1.35
Ensure	Approach	1.25
Transmit	Torque	1.32
Withstand	Torque	3.68
Prevent	Rusting	1.25
Join	Components	1.89
Receive	Torque	1.56
Facilitate	Grip	1.00
Improve	Aesthetics	0.16
	Total	13.46

7.1.5 Technically Oriented FAST Diagram

The technical FAST Diagram of the screwdriver is shown in Fig. 7.2.

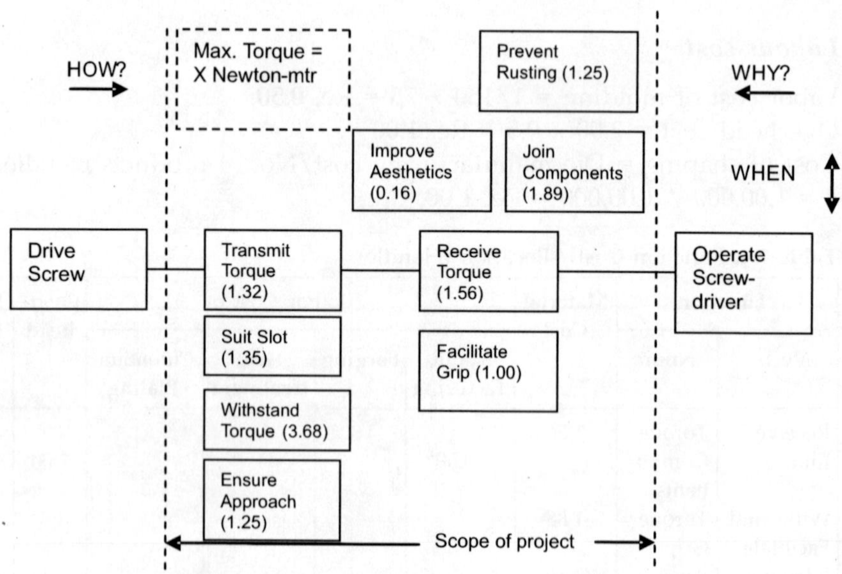

Fig. 7.2. Technically Oriented FAST Diagram.

7.2 VALUE INDEX AND VALUE GAP

Value index is the ratio of the worth and the total cost. In the technical FAST diagram, the functions on the critical path are the only functions which can together (including basic function) fulfill the higher order function. Hence, worth of the project is the summation of cost of all the functions on the critical path.

In the above example, the worth of the project is Rs. 2.88 and the total cost is Rs. 13.46. So, the value index of the project is 2.88/13.46 is 0.21. The value gap will be Rs. 13.46–2.88 = Rs. 10.58.

The value index is less and the value gap in monetary terms is quite high which indicates that there is enormous potential for improvement.

The author advocates usage of the value gap, rather than value index, because it gives better indicators in terms of monetary savings.

7.3 RATIO ANALYSIS

Ratio analysis is extensively used in analyzing financial data. Here, the ratio analysis can be used to identify the unnecessary cost areas. The following may be the possible ratios which can be used as indicators:

1. Basic function cost to total cost
2. Value index
3. All time functions' cost to total cost
4. One-time function cost to total cost
5. At the same time functions' cost to total cost

7.3.1 Basic Function Cost to Total Cost

This is the ratio of basic function cost of the existing product/process/system with the total cost of product/process/system. This will indicate how much cost has been spent on the basic function.

In the above example, the ratio comes to 0.098 (1.32/13.46). That is, less than ten percent has been spent on the basic function for which the item has been created. That means because of the design aspect the cost of the product has increased.

So this will force the team to concentrate on the design aspect as well as evaluate other aspects.

7.3.2 Value Index or Value Gap

There is a specific method of finding out the worth of the project, through function-cost-worth matrix. In the Technically Oriented FAST Diagramming Model too, one can find out the worth of the project. Here, in this model the functions on the critical path are only responsible for achieving the basic function and also responsible to achieve the higher order function. Hence, the total cost of the functions in the critical path within the scope of the project, is the worth of the project. And the total cost of the project is the summation of all the costs of the functions within the scope of the project.

So, one can find out the value index by the ratio of worth by total cost. The ratio will indicate whether the project is cost effective or something needs to be done to improve its cost effectiveness.

In the above example, the value index is 0.21. So there is lot of scope to improve the project.

7.3.3 All Time Functions' Cost to Total Cost

The "all the time functions" arise from the design aspects of the project. These "all time functions" are mapped in the FAST diagram on the top right hand corner. If these costs are added, it will indicate the cost of the "all the time functions". The ratio of "all time functions' cost" to the total cost will indicate how much cost has been included because of a particular design consideration. Lower the ratio, better it is.

The ratio may help the team to pinpoint the potential areas for improvement. For the above example the ratio comes to (3.30/13.46 = 0.25).

7.3.4 One Time Function Cost to Total Cost

This ratio may not be available in the system. However, the team members should concentrate on this ratio, because this may be a qualitative component of the system. This can be helpful for selling the product. The team can reduce the cost and improve this item which may improve future revenue.

7.3.5 At The Same Time Functions' Cost to Total Cost

This is a ratio of the summation of all "at the same time functions" to the total cost. In the above example the ratio is 0.54 (7.28/13.46). This appears to be high and the team should go into the details.

It may be worthwhile to mention that the team can decide the budgeted ratio of each ratio and work on that basis.

7.4 EXERCISE

1. **The product cost of an item has to be transformed into**
   (a) Production cost (b) Work cost
   (c) Function cost (d) Total cost

2. **The process of allocation of cost is to**
   (a) Start allocation from lower order function
   (b) Start with basic function
   (c) Start with higher order function
   (d) Hold functions in isolation of each other

3. **What is not considered the basic rule of allocation?**
   (a) Select the team
   (b) Select one function first.
   (c) Find out a comparable item that does not have the other functions.
   (d) Determine the cost of that item. This cost will be the functional cost of the first function.

CHAPTER

8

Case Studies

"The greater danger for most of us is not that our aim is too high and we missed it, but that is too low and we reached it."

– Michelangelo, Italian Painter, Sculpture, Architect and Poet (1475-1568)

Case Study: 1

Innovative Ideas for Design Optimization of Fifth Wheel Coupling

8.1 MOUNTING STRUCTURE

8.1.1 Information Phase

Fifth wheel coupling is used for the purpose of coupling the tractor with trailer. With this mechanism, the tractor pulls the trailer.

8.1.2 Function Phase

8.1.2.1 Functional Analysis

Function analysis of the fifth wheel coupling mounting structure is given in Table 8.1. Initially, the function of the assembly is done, then the functions of the components. Each component will have basic function and may have some secondary functions. All should be mentioned in the column provided for that.

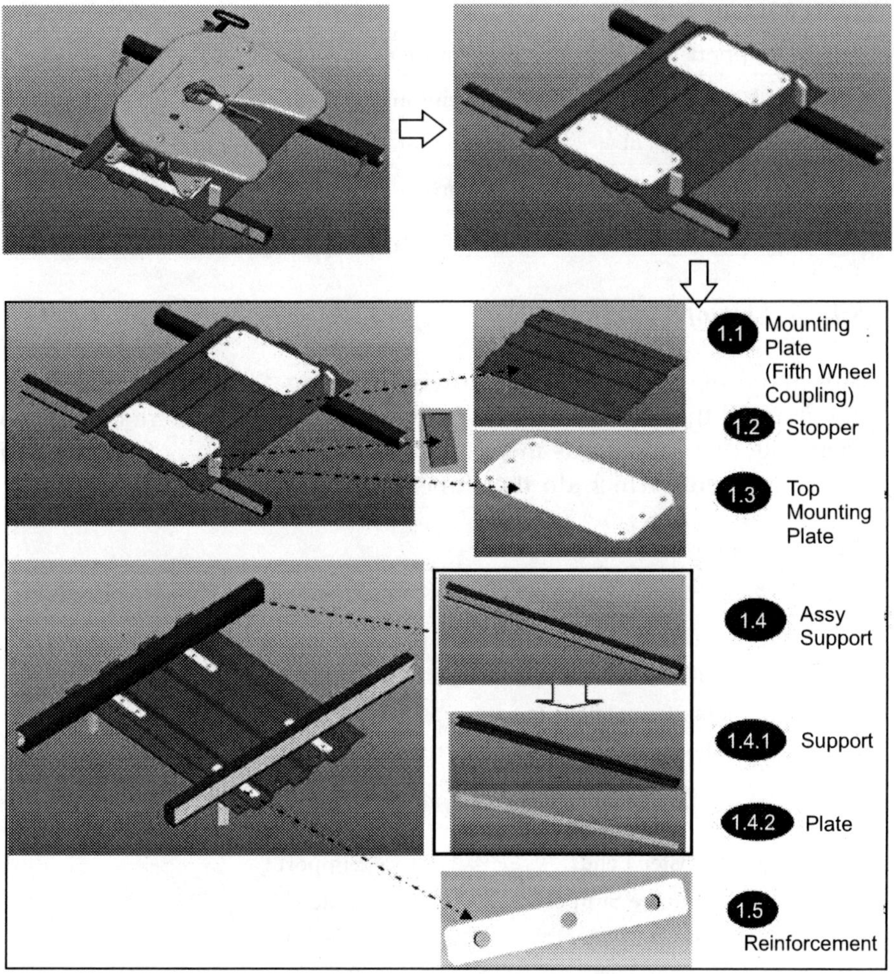

Table 8.1: Function Analysis of Fifth Wheel Coupling Mounting Structure

Sr. No.	Components	Function		Basic/ Secondary
		Verb	**Noun**	
1	Assembly Mounting plate (Fifth Wheel Coupling)	Accommodate	Components	Basic
1.1	Mounting Plate	Accommodate	Components	Basic
	Withstand	Load	Secondary	
	Maintain	Height	Secondary	
	Position	Components	Secondary	
1.2	Stopper	Check	Deflection	Basic
1.3	Top Mounting Plate	Facilitate	Mounting	Basic
		Reinforce	Mounting Plate	Basic

Contd.

Table 8.1: Contd.

1.4.1	Support	Transfer	Load	Basic
1.4.2	Plate	Reinforce	Support	Basic
1.5	Reinforcement	Reinforce	Mounting Plate	Basic
1.6	Welding	Join	Components	Basic
1.7	Paint	Prevent	Rust	Basic

8.1.2.2 List of Functions

Summary of functions are shown in Table 8.2. While making the summary, if the same function is being executed by different components, then only one function is mentioned, but the mention is to be made for the components which do that function.

Table 8.2: Summary of Functions

Sr. No.	Function	Components
1	Accommodate Components	Mounting Plate
2	Withstand Load	Mounting Plate
3	Maintain Height	Mounting Plate
4	Check Deflection	Stopper
5	Facilitate Mounting	Top Mounting Plate
6	Reinforce Mounting Plate	Top Mounting Plate; Reinforcement
7	Transfer Load	Support
8	Reinforce Support	Plate
9	Join Components	Welding
10	Prevent Rust	Paint
11	Position Components	Mounting Plate

8.1.2.3 Functional Analysis System Technique (FAST)

Based on the summary of functions, the following two types of FAST diagrams have been drawn.

1. Technically Oriented FAST Diagram
2. Customer-Oriented FAST Diagram

1. *Technically Oriented FAST Diagram:* In order to draw the Technically Oriented FAST diagram, it has to be decided which function appears to the basic function. In this case it appears to be basic function, i.e., 'accommodate components". These components are put in a block and question asked: "Why" which is shown below.

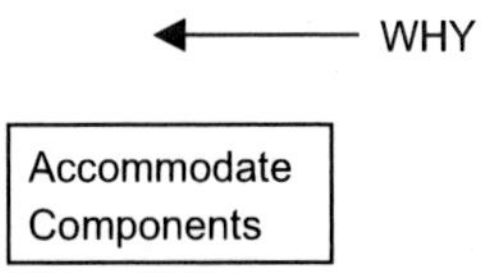

Fig. 8.1.

The answer to Why, will provide the higher order function. In this case it is "secure connection". Putting the function "secure connection" inside the block, as shown in Fig. 8.2.

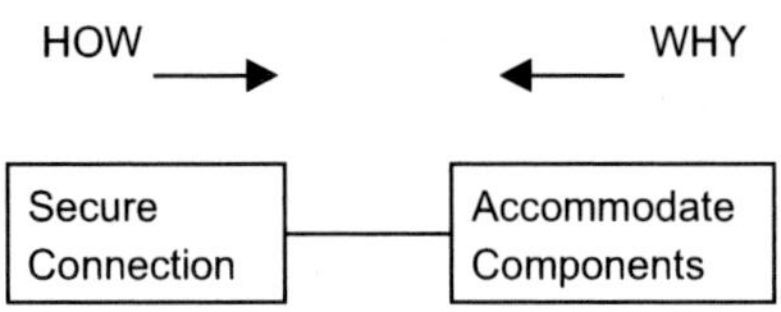

Fig. 8.2.

In order to validate the position of the "secure connection" function, the "How" question is used. If the answer gives the right hand function then the position is proper and valid. Here answer of how to "secure connections" is given as "accommodate components", hence the positioning is correct and the "secure connection" is the higher order function and the basic function is "accommodate components". A dotted scope line is drawn to make the left boundary line of the project.

Now, questioning "How" to "accommodate components" , the next function on the right side of basic function will come and it has to be validated by "Why". Here it will be "position components".

On the same basis the functions on the critical path are finalized. The function which is not part of the project is the lower order function. A right scope line of the project is drawn. This is shown in Fig. 8.3.

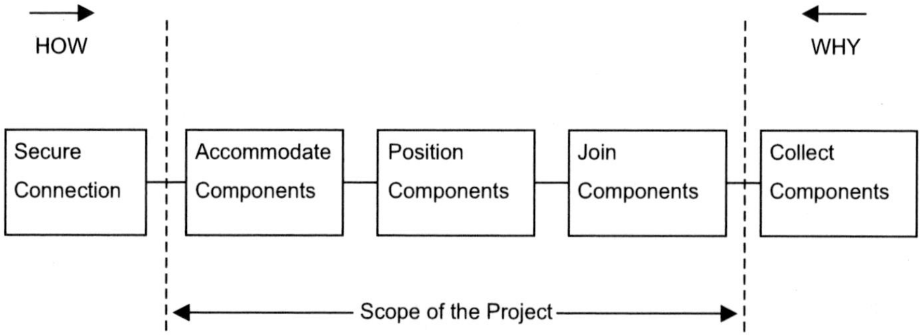

Fig. 8.3.

The next step of drawing the diagram is to find out against each functions in the critical path (Excepting H.O.F. AND L.O.F.) and any other function which happens "At The Same Time" or "Caused by" that function of the critical path. In this example, the function "Withstand Load" should happen "At the Same Time" when "Accommodate Components" happens. Similarly, the function "Transfer Load" happens "At the Same Time" when "Join components" happens. The new diagram is shown in Fig. 8.4.

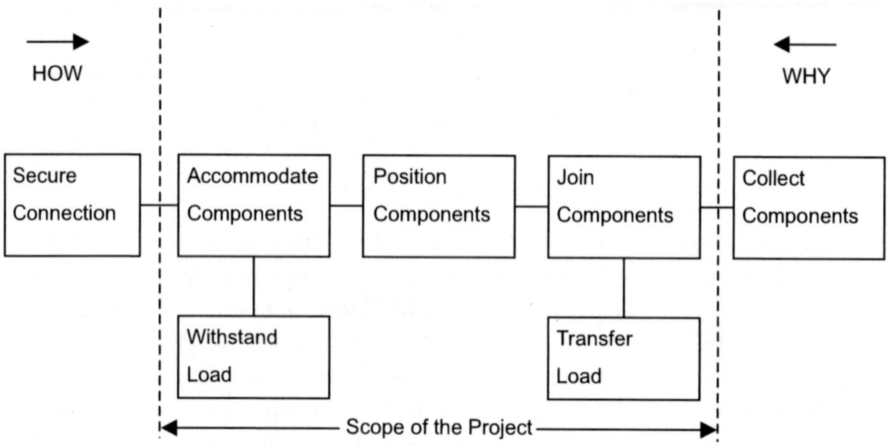

Fig. 8.4.

The next step is to place the design objective in the diagram. It is shown in Fig. 8.5.

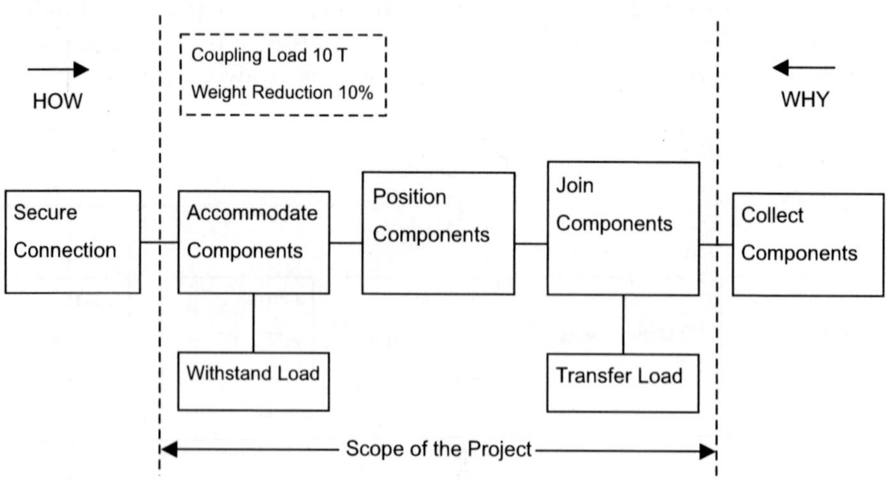

Fig. 8.5.

The last step will be the placement of "All The Time Functions" and "One Time Function", if any. The final diagram is shown in Fig. 8.6.

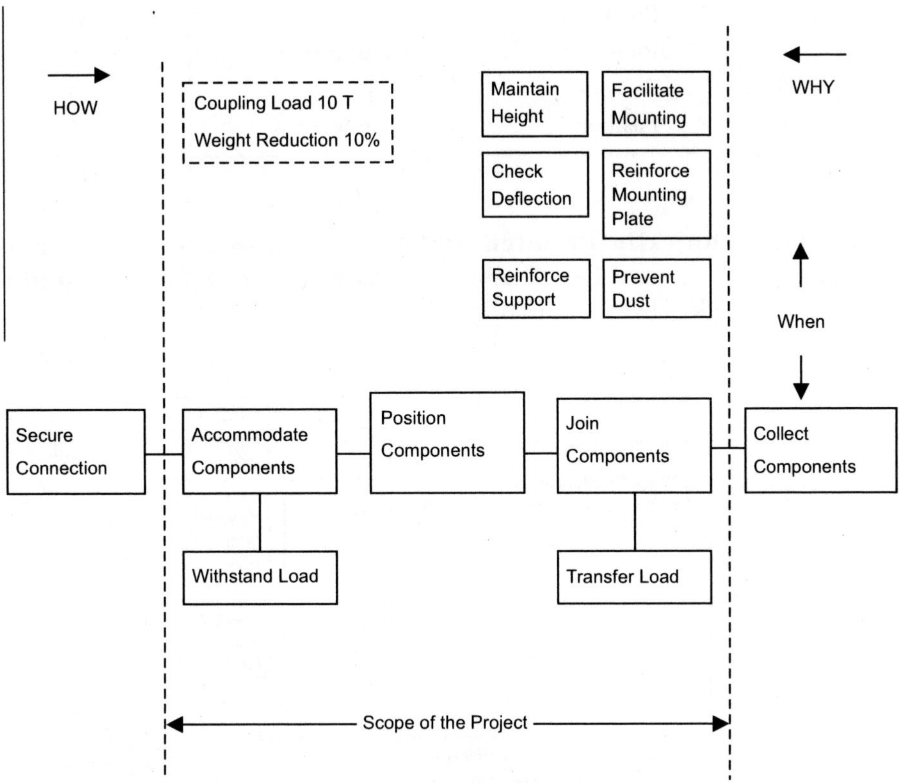

Fig. 8.6.

Function cost allocation: In value methodology function is the heart. To quote L.D. Miles "All cost is for functions". The product cost has to be converted into function cost. The product cost of the components has to be converted into function cost as shown in Table 8.3.

Table 8.3: Function Cost Allocation Matrix

Sr. No.	Function		Function Cost
	Verb	Noun	
1	Accommodate	Components	600
2	Withstand	Load	1030
3	Maintain	Height	412
4	Check	Deflection	69
5	Facilitate	Mounting	294
6	Reinforce	Mounting Plate	196

Contd.

Table 8.3: Contd.

7	Transfer	Load	780
8	Reinforce	Support	334
9	Join	Components	166
10	Prevent	Rust	249
11	Position	Components	18
		Total	4148

Revisit technically oriented FAST: Now with function cost, the Technically Oriented Fast Diagram is redrawn with function cost in the function block. This is shown in Fig. 8.7.

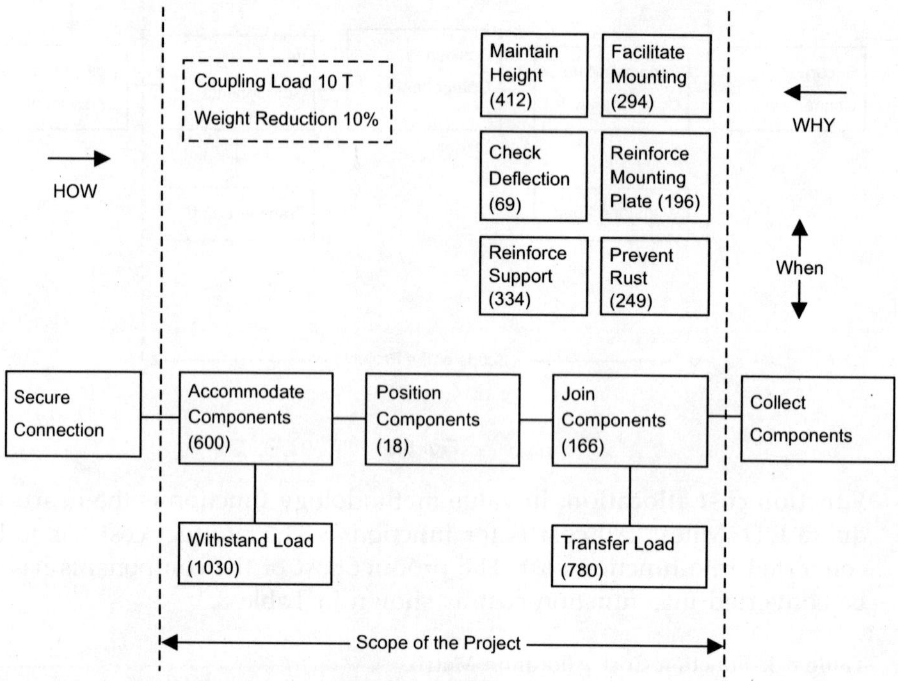

Fig. 8.7.

Value index: The value index is a measure to indicate the potential of the value study. In the Technically Oriented FAST Diagram, the value index can be defined as the ratio of total cost of the project to total cost of functions on the critical path, because the critical path functions are the bare minimum functions required to achieve the objective which is higher order function. This can be represented as below:

$$\text{Value Index} = \frac{\text{Cost of total project}}{\text{Cost of the critical path functions}}$$

In the present case studies, the value index will be calculated as below:

$$\text{Value index} = \frac{4148}{784} = 5.29$$

The cost of the total project should be as nearer as the cost of the critical path functions. Value index under 2.00 is a good target. (Source: *Function Approach to Transportation Project* by Muthaih Kasi)

2. *Customer-Oriented FAST Diagram:* A Customer-Oriented FAST Diagram is based suited during the planning stage of the project. The objective is to connect tractor with trailor. The connection between the two is important from safety point of view. The "task" of the project should be "secure connection" By asking question of "How" the first level of primary function can be obtained. This is shown in Fig. 8.8.

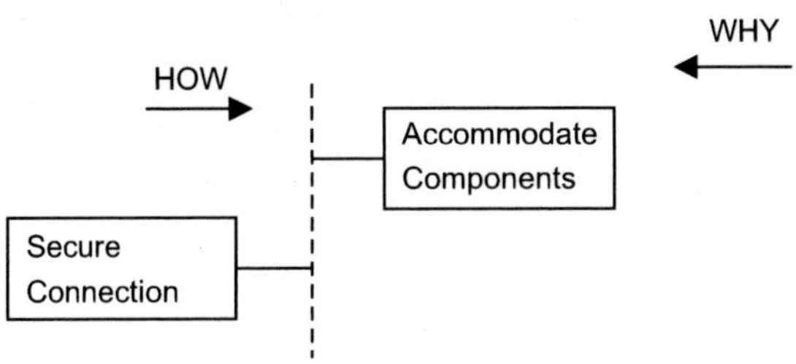

Fig. 8.8.

The next step is to ask "How?" to the first level of primary function, that is "accommodate components", the two functions "position components" and "join components" are branched out. Figure 8.9 shows the second level of primary function.

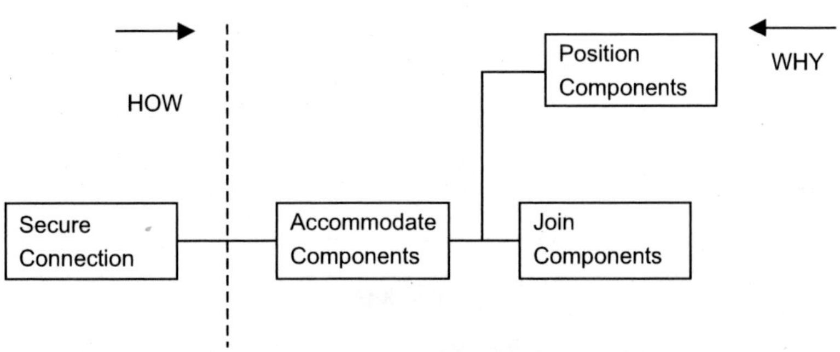

Fig. 8.9.

Supporting Functions

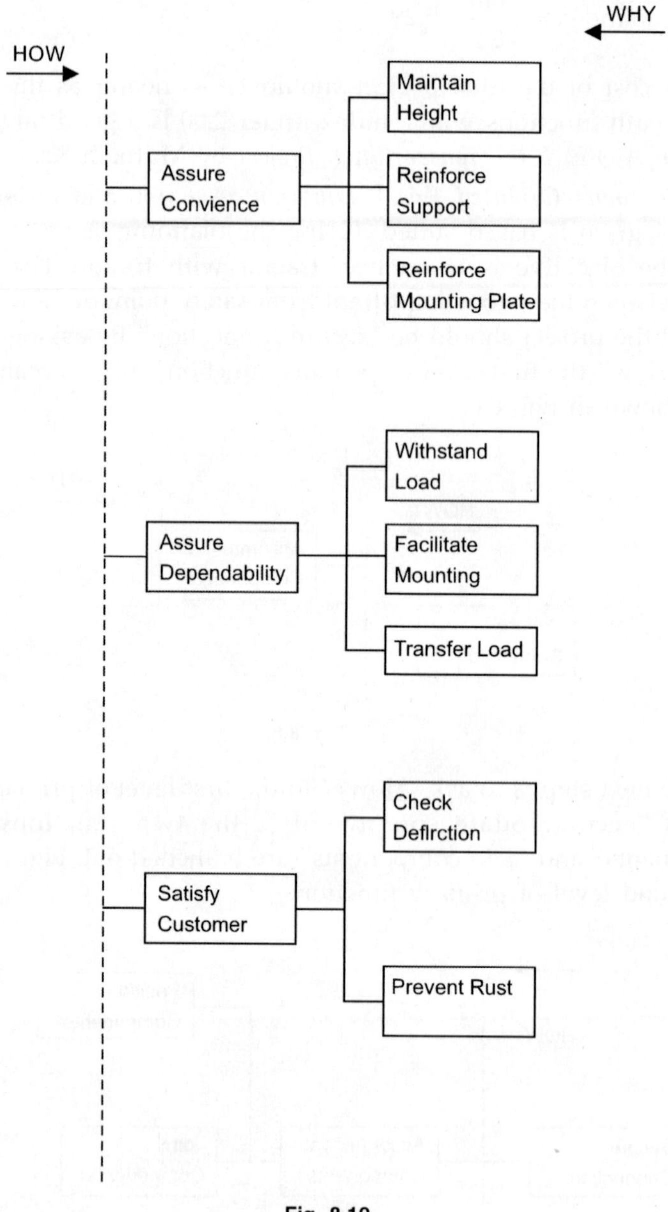

Fig. 8.10.

Revisit customer-oriented FAST: Now with function cost, the Customer-Oriented Fast Diagram is redrawn with function cost in the function block. This is shown in Fig. 8.11.

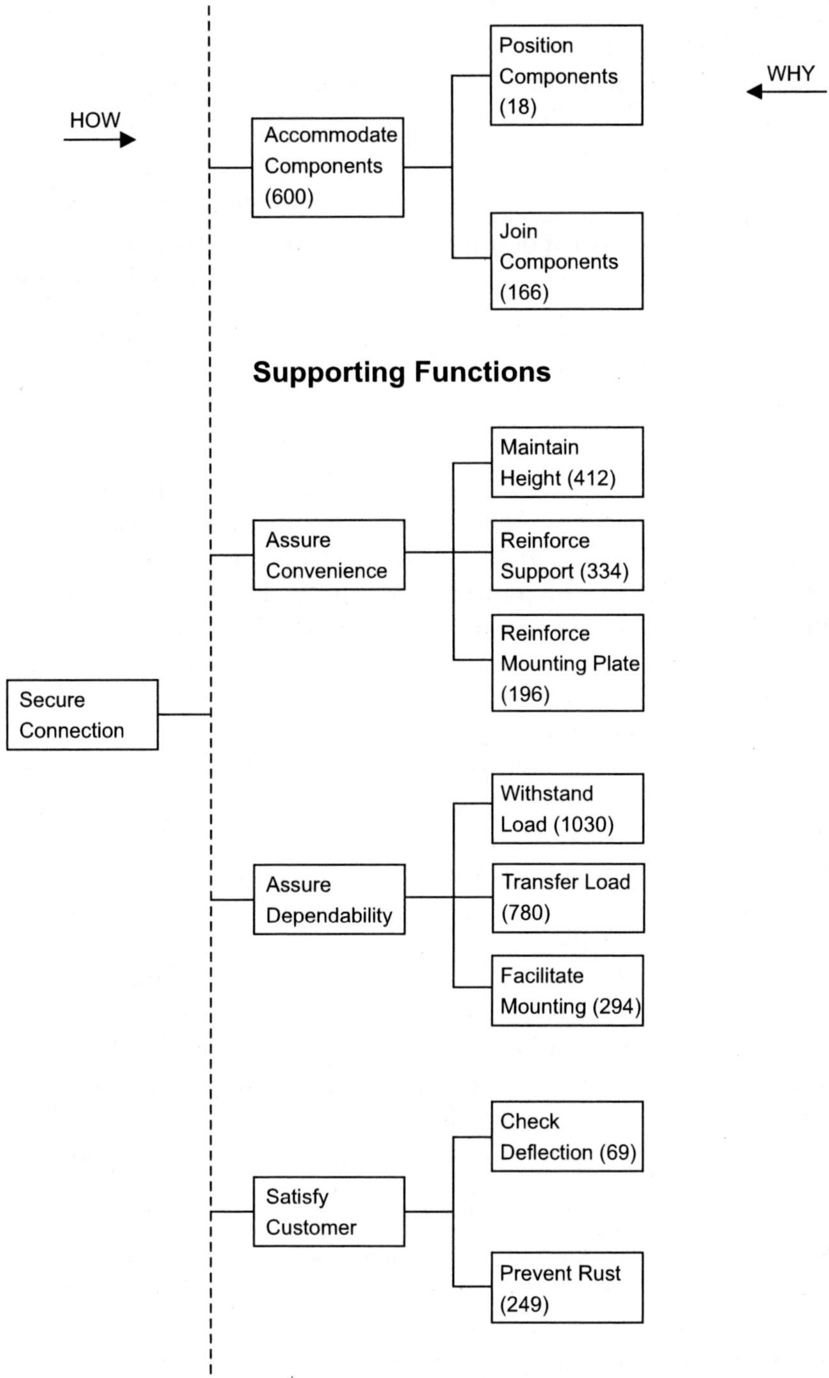
HOW
WHY
Accommodate Components (600)
Position Components (18)
Join Components (166)
Supporting Functions
Assure Convenience
Maintain Height (412)
Reinforce Support (334)
Reinforce Mounting Plate (196)
Secure Connection
Assure Dependability
Withstand Load (1030)
Transfer Load (780)
Facilitate Mounting (294)
Satisfy Customer
Check Deflection (69)
Prevent Rust (249)

Fig. 8.11.

Value index: The value index is a measure to indicate the potential of the value study. In the Customer-Oriented FAST Diagram, the value index can be defined as the ratio of total cost of the project to cost of primary functions and cost of assure dependable functions. This can be represented as below:

$$\text{Value index} = \frac{\text{Cost of total project}}{(\text{Cost of primary functions} + \text{Cost of assure dependable functions})}$$

In the present case studies, the value index will be calculated as below:

$$\text{Value index} = \frac{4148}{2888} = 1.44$$

The cost of the total project should be as nearer as the cost of primary functions plus cost of assure dependable functions. (Source: *Function Approach to Transportation Project* by Muthaih Kasi)

How to use FAST diagram for creativity: In the VM job plan each phase is a process. As the characteristic of process it must have input and there will be output, which will become input to the next phase. The next phase of job plan after function phase is the creative phase. The expert's advise is as below:

Charles W. Bytheway has mentioned in his book "FAST Creativity and Innovation". I quote from his book,

"One of the best ways to approach the brainstorming task is to post the primary path functions along with the parts that actually perform those functions—used the Charles Kettering approach, where we imagine ourselves as one of the parts."

Muthiah Kasi has also mentioned in his book "Function Approach to Transportation Projects". I quote from his book,

"Ideas can be generated by functions. The "How" and "Why" logic critical path will give functions a different level of logical thinking. Using these functions, similar ideas can be generated."

Table 8.4 Generation of creative ideas is used for generating ideas.

Table 8.4: Generation of Creative Ideas

Sr. No.	Functions on the Critical Path	Components responsible Creative Ideas for Functions
1	Accommodate Components	Mounting Plate
2	Position Components	Mounting Plate
3	Join Components	Welding

Case Study: 2

Study of Corridor Availability for 33 kV Power Transmission

8.2 INFORMATION PHASE

8.2.1 The following are the stakeholders of the project.

1. Iron ore mines
2. Logistics and loading of the iron ores.
3. Ferroalloy plant

8.2.2 Define Stakeholders' Constraints / Needs / Desires

The following is the list of constraints, needs and desires (C/N/D) in Table 8.5.

Table 8.5: Statement of Constraint/Need/Desire of Stakeholders

Sr. No.	Statements	Code
1	Availability of power	N
2	Production of iron ore and convey to destination	D
3	Power availability	C
4	RLS construction	N
5	Land availability	C
6	Loading of iron ore	D
7	Railway track laying	N
8	Peripheral road construction	N
9	Dispatch iron ore to KPO	D
10	Dumping sludge in "As is where is" condition	N
11	No interruption in dumping of sludge	D
12	Land availability	C
13	Retain dump yard	N
14	No damage to retaining wall	D
15	C&W plant operation	N
16	OLCS to convey iron ore	N

8.2.3 Function Analysis

The following is the list of functions related to power transmission, dispatch iron ore, dump sludge in Table 8.6 to Table 8.8.

Table 8.6: Power Transmission

Sr. No.	Functions	
	Verb	**Noun**
1	Transmit	Power
2	Maintain	Voltage
3	Connect	Source
4	Prevent	Accident
5	Create	Corridor
6	Produce	Passageway
7	Support	Weight (High Tension Cable)

Table 8.7: Dispatch Iron Ore

Sr. No.	Functions	
	Verb	**Noun**
1	Create	Loading Area
2	Aid	Movement
3	Facilitate	Approach
4	Retain	Underground Utilities

Table 8.8: Dump Sludge

Sr. No.	Functions	
	Verb	**Noun**
1	Dump	Sludge
2	Secure	Access
3	Retain	Sludge
4	Preserve	Old Tower
5	Secure	Retaining Wall
6	Restrict	Dump Height
7	Prevent	Accident
8	Prevent	Contamination

8.2.4 Summary of Functions

The value methodology is concerned with functions. Function analysis, as above, is generated against a particular item. It is clear that one function can be achieved through two or more items. Based on that the following summary is made where only functions are mentioned as in Table 8.9.

Table 8.9: Summary of Functions

Sr. No.	Functions	
	Verb	**Noun**
1	Transmit	Power
2	Maintain	Voltage
3	Connect	Source
4	Prevent	Accident
5	Create	Corridor
6	Produce	Passageway
7	Support	Weight (High Tension Cable)
8	Create	Loading Area
9	Aid	Movement
10	Facilitate	Approach
11	Retain	Underground Utilities
12	Dump	Sludge
13	Secure	Access
14	Maintain	Sludge
15	Preserve	Old Tower
16	Retain	Wall
17	Restrict	Dump Height
18	Prevent	Contamination

8.2.5 Functional Analysis System Technique (FAST)

Based on the summary of functions, the following two types of FAST diagrams have been drawn.

1. Technically Oriented FAST Diagram
2. Customer-Oriented FAST Diagram

8.2.5.1 Technically Oriented FAST Diagram

The first step is to find out which function is the basic function. The team finalizes that "Appears to be the Basic Function" is Transmit Power.

Asking question of "Why", the team finalizes as "Receive Power". Asking question to "How" to receive power the answer is "Transmit Power". Now, both the functions are validated by 'Why' and 'How' questions.

Hence, the higher order function is 'Receive Power'. Asking 'How' question the team finalizes the required secondary functions on the critical path. Each function's placement should be validated by 'Why' question. The function which is not a part of the project will be lower order function/assumed function/causative function. The critical path functions are shown in Fig. 8.12.

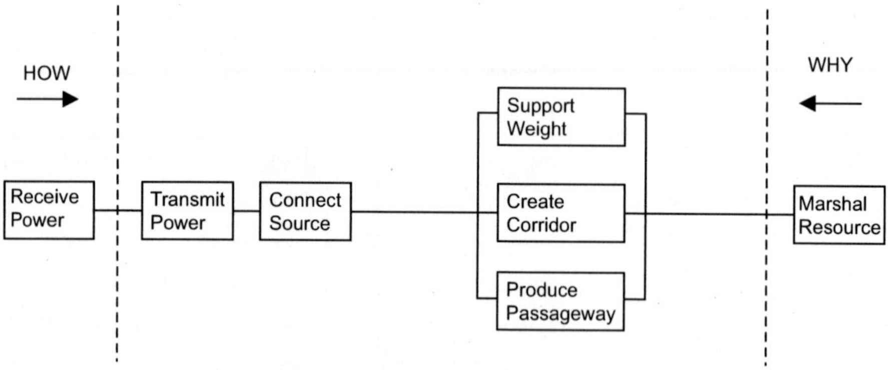

Fig. 8.12.

The next step will be to decide the design objectives of the project. These are:

1. Cater 33 MVA load
2. Corridor length 510 m

Putting the design objectives' blocks in proper place the FAST diagram will look like as shown in Fig. 8.13.

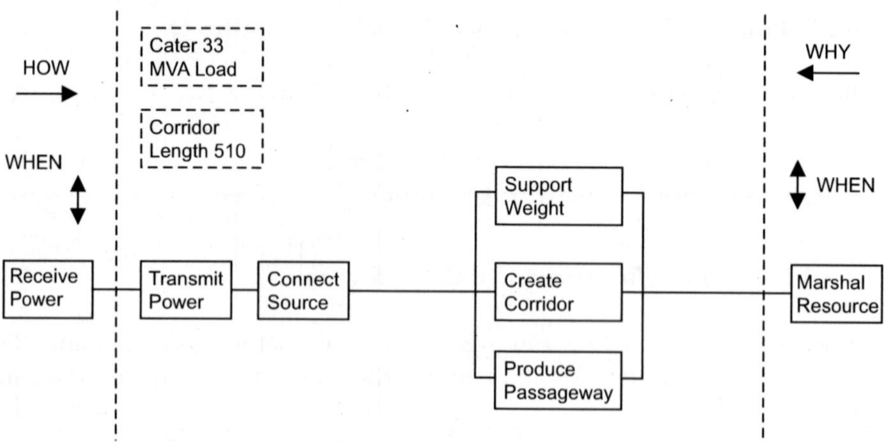

Fig. 8.13.

It is to be identified now whether there is any function which is considered "At the same time" or "Caused by the function" from the list of functions shown in Table 8.2.5. There is only one function "Maintain Voltage" which is happening when the function "Transmit Power" is happening.

There may be some functions which happen once in the life time of the product. Those functions are called 'One Time Functions'. It is not necessary that there will be one time function at the same time there may be more than one function a 'One time function'. The dedicated slot for 'One time function' is beside the design objectives. If more than one, it may be put in vertically. Figure 8.14 will indicate both the above types of functions.

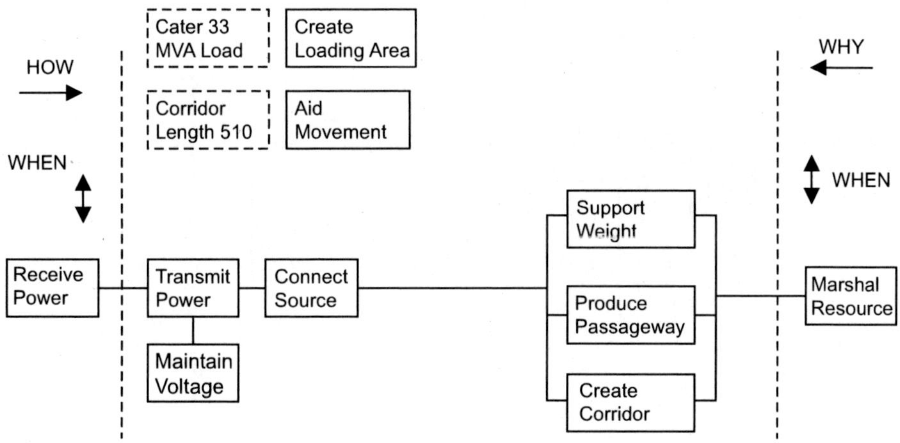

Fig. 8.14.

The last bunch of functions which is known as 'all the time functions' should be identified and be placed on the left side of right scope line above the critical path. This is shown as in Fig. 8.15.

8.2.5.2 Customer-Oriented FAST Diagram

In Customer-Oriented FAST, the first step is to identify the TASK. In this example the TASK is "Receive power'. Now by questioning 'How' logic the next function, which will be a primary function is to be identified. It will be 'Transmit Power'. This function has to be validated by asking 'Why' question to 'Transmit Power'. The answer comes as 'Receive power'. Hence, the position of functions is finalized. Next question 'How' is asked to 'Transmit Power'. Now three functions 'Maintain Voltage', 'Connect Source' and 'Install Medium' will be

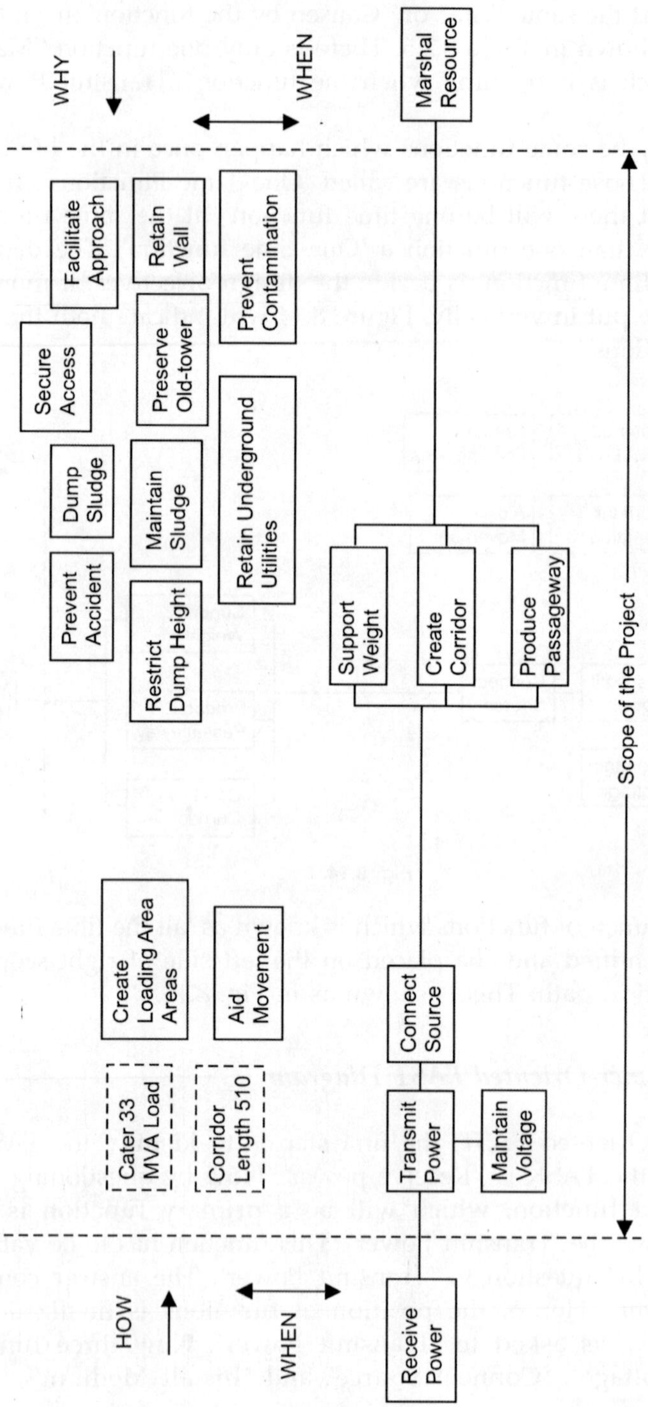
WHY
WHEN
HOW
WHEN
Receive Power
Transmit Power
Maintain Voltage
Connect Source
Cater 33 MVA Load
Corridor Length 510
Create Loading Area Areas
Aid Movement
Support Weight
Create Corridor
Produce Passageway
Prevent Accident
Dump Sludge
Secure Access
Facilitate Approach
Restrict Dump Height
Maintain Sludge
Preserve Old-tower
Retain Wall
Retain Underground Utilities
Prevent Contamination
Marshal Resource
Scope of the Project

Fig. 8.15.

the answers. All the three functions are validated through question 'Why'. This functions is in the primary function line which is shown in Fig. 8.16.

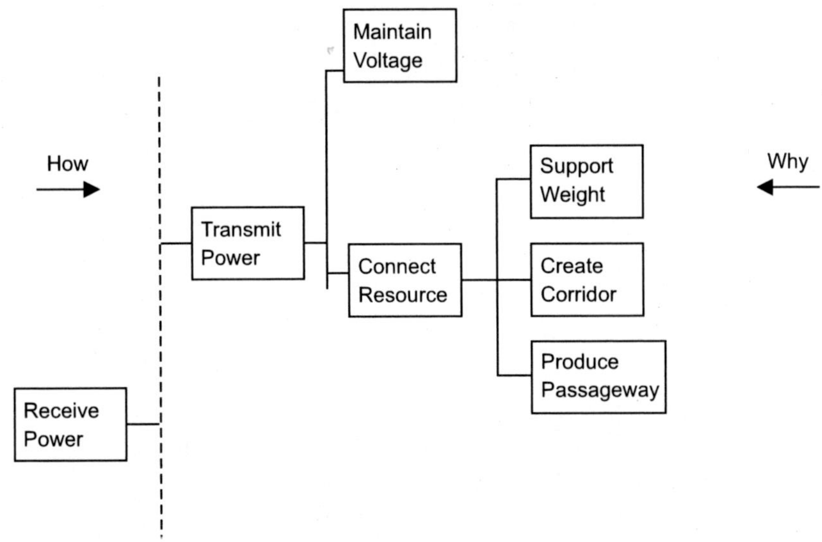

Fig. 8.16.

The next step is to identify the supporting functions. The first supporting function is 'Assure Convenience'. The following functions are identified which provide convenience to the customers. Similarly, Assure Dependability and Satisfy Customer in Fig. 8.17.

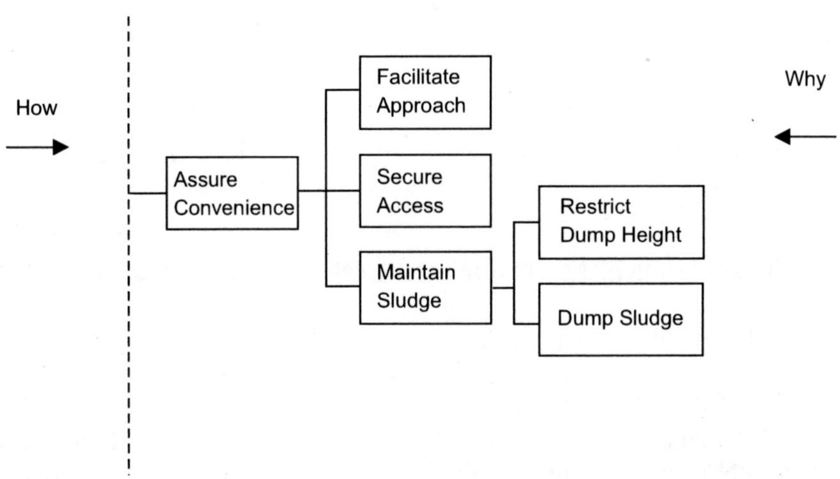

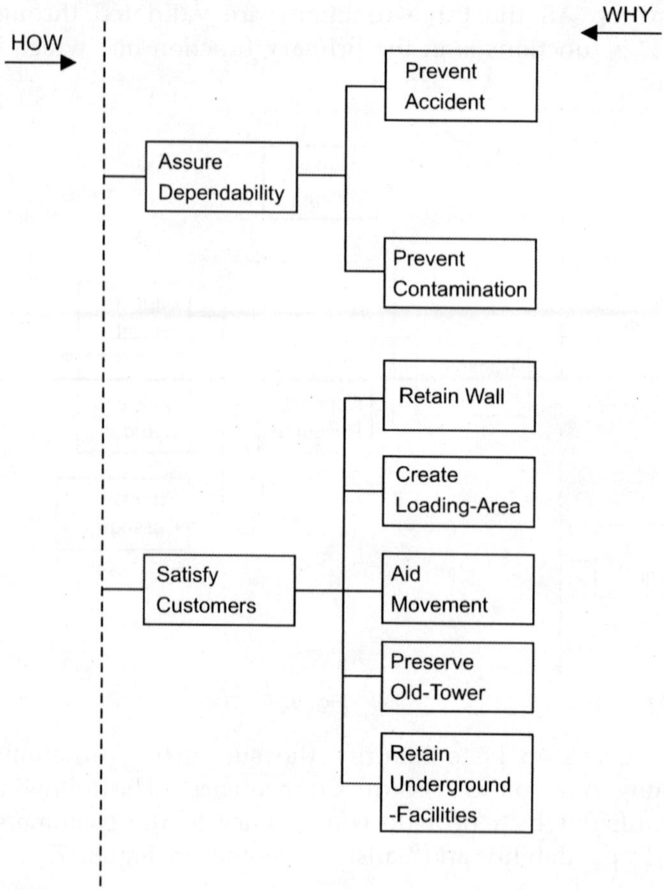

Fig. 8.17.

Case Study: 3

Value Engineering Study on "Slurry Outflow during Column Concreting".

8.3 EFFECTIVE EXECUTION OF COLUMN CONCRETING

8.3.1 Study Objective

In view of this, different studies were done to see the areas contributing to unnecessary costs. We found out one such area as the slurry outflow during column concreting. Columns constitute an important portion in the structural components of a building. A value engineering study was done for the effective execution of column concreting.

8.3.2 Orientation Phase

Table 8.10: Input-Process-Output Matrix

Input	Process	Output
Resort to Value Methodology	Orientation Phase	1. VM Training 2. Team Selection 3. Project Selection

8.3.2.1 Value Engineering Team

The VE team consisted of engineers from various departments. It was a balanced multidisciplinary team.

Team Members Designation Department

1. Xxxxx Senior Engineer, Project 'X'
2. xxxxxx Senior Engineer, Project 'Y'
3. xxxxx Engineer, Project 'Z'
4. xxxxx Project Engineer, Projects 'X'
5. xxxxxx Senior Engineer, Value Engineering
6. Team Leader: xxxxx
7. Team Facilitator: xxxxx

8.3.3 Project Selection

Slurry outflow during column concreting.

8.3.4 Information Phase

In this phase all possible information regarding the process of column concreting was gathered.

First, the column starters are fixed to make sure that the columns are located at the right place and are correctly aligned according to the construction drawings. Steel starter molds are used preferably. As per standard practice, the size of the starter should always be 1 mm smaller on all the sides to prevent the starter from cracking and to accommodate the foam strip, while fixing the column formwork.

The area where the starter mold is fixed should be cleaned properly. The column is located and the starter is marked with respect to the grid lines and fixed by bolting. The starter is checked diagonally to ensure right angles.

Fig. 8.18. Starter Installation.

Rods are tied to the column reinforcement above the starter mold at suitable intervals. Wedges are driven in between these rods and starter, to hold the mold firmly in position during concreting. Curing is done for the starter. Reinforcement fixing for the columns should be checked with respect to the GFC drawings. The cover blocks have to be tied to the reinforcement rods as per specifications. The area around the starter where the shuttering box to be fixed should be clean and smooth to facilitate easy fixing of the column formwork. Foam strips to be placed around the starter and the shuttering box sides for the longer side of the column are brought into place at the starter. The verticality is checked using a plumb bob on its external face and the sides. The shuttering box is temporarily tied to the column reinforcement to keep it in place.

Fig. 8.19. Shuttering Arrangement.

Then the sides corresponding to the shorter sides of the columns are brought into place and the plumb is checked.

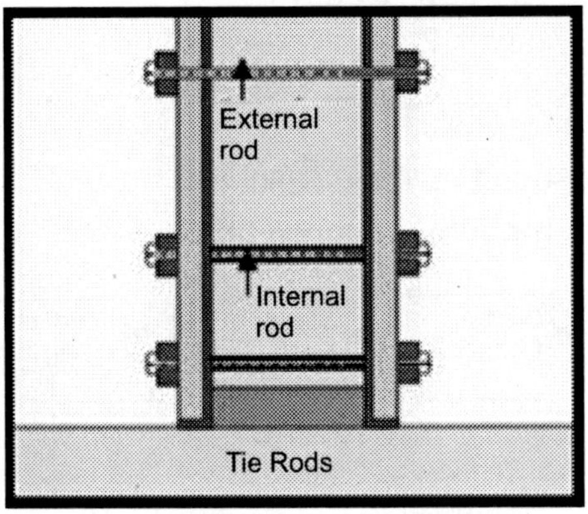

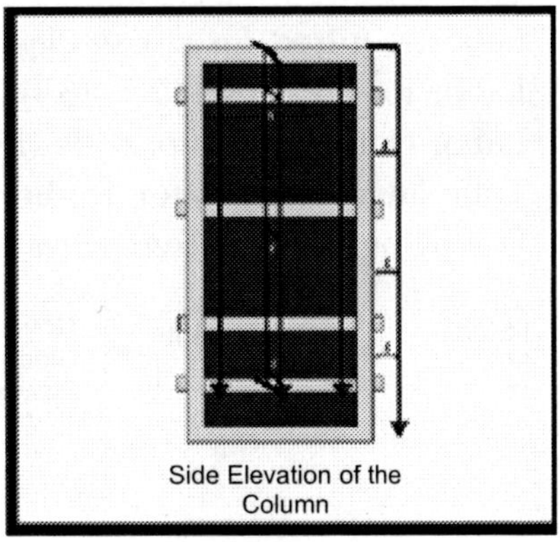

Fig. 8.20. Fixing of Tie Rods

The external tie rods which do not pass through the concrete, connecting the two longer sides of the column shuttering are fixed (20 mm dia). Then the internal tie rods (16 mm dia) which pass through the concrete are fixed. These tie rods will pass through PVC pipes within the column concrete which facilitate easy removal of the tie rods during deshuttering. Steel bracing pipes are fixed on both sides of the column through which the tie rod comes out. The plumb is checked once again for the longer and shorter sides. The plumb bob is tied from the top at a distance from the column box using a small iron rod. Then concreting is done. Alignment checking to be done at constant intervals.

The problem of slurry leakage happens in first as well as in the second lifts of column shuttering during concreting. There are various reasons for the slurry outflow. It may be due to the displacement of tie rod holes, undulations in shuttering materials, improper placement of foam sheets. The slurry outflow results in one more activity of cleaning or chipping off the slurry soon after concreting. The standard height of shuttering materials is 2.44 m. The floor to floor height for floors other than basement is 2.975 m. The problem of slurry outflow mainly arises in the basement as the floor to floor height is more than one column shuttering box height.

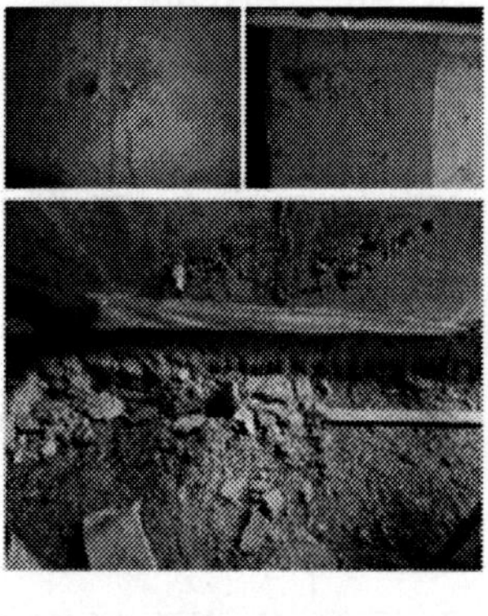

Costing details:

The labor cost for slurry cleaning is very high.
Time required for casting 50 columns= app. 15 days
Labor required for slurry cleaning/day = 2
Labor for 15 days = 2 × 15 = 30
Labor charges per no: = Rs. 175
Total labor charges for 15 days = 30 × 175 = Rs. 5250
Following is the activity flowchart for column concreting:

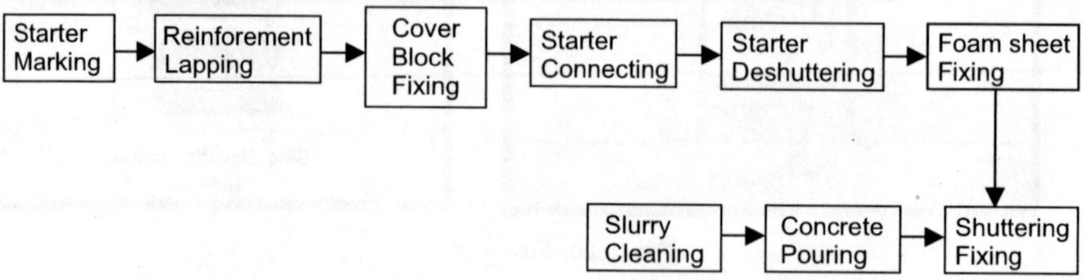

Fig. 8.21. Activity Flowchart for Column Concreting (Change Alignment).

Table 8.11: Input Process Output Matrix

Input	Process	Output
Project Selection the	Information Phase	Detailed adequate information for Project.

8.3.5 Function Phase

8.3.5.1 Function Listing

The various sub-activities involved in column concreting are defined and listed below along with their basic and secondary functions.

Table 8.12. Function Analysis

Sr. No.	Activity	Function		
		Verb	Noun	B/S
1	Starter Marking	Maintain Confirm Preserve Guarantee Secure	Alignment Shape Safety Quality Position	B S S S S
2	Reinforcement Lapping	Enhance Assure	Strength Cleanliness	B S
3	Cover Block Fixing	Prevent Prevent	Exposure Corrosion	B S

4	Starter Concreting	Hold Maintain	Shuttering Alignment	B S
5	Deshuttering	Expose Facilitate	Surface Fixing (Foam Sheet)	B S
6	Foam Sheet Fixing	Minimize Minimize Ensure	Leakage Clean up Grip	B S S
7	Shutter Fixing	Secure Connect Maintain Prevent	Forms Components Integrity Injury	B S S S
8	Concrete Pouring	Transfer Cast Contain Flow Create Enhance	Load Component Slurry Material Boundary Strength	B S S S S S
9	Slurry Cleaning	Improve Maximize Produce	Finish Appearance Debris	B S S

Table 8.13: Summary of Functions

Basic Functions		**Secondary Functions**	
Prevent	Exposure	Confirm	Shape
Hold	Shuttering	Preserve	Safety
Expose	Surface	Guarantee	Quality
Minimize	Leakage	Secure	Position
Secure	Forms	Assure	Cleanliness
Transfer	Load	Prevent	Corrosion
Improve	Finish	Prevent	Corrosion
		Maintain	Alignment
		Facilitate	Fixing (Foam Sheet)
		Minimize	Clean up
		Ensure	Grip
		Connect	Components
		Maintain	Integrity
		Prevent	Injury
		Cast	Component
		Contain	Slurry
		Flow	Material
		Create	Boundary
		Enhance	Strength
		Maximize	Appearance
		Produce	Debris

8.3.5.2 Technical FAST

The technical FAST is to be drawn based on the functions mentioned in Table 8.13. The following steps are followed.

1. Decide which function appears to be a basic function.
2. Ask question "Why" to the "Appears to be the Basic Function"
3. The answer should be placed on the left side of the "Appears to be the Basic Function".
4. Get it validated by asking question "How" to the new function. If the validation is accepted then the new function is the higher order function. Now "Appears to be the Basic Function" will become the basic function of the project.
5. Ask question 'How' to basic function and pinpoint a function from the random list of functions. Asking 'Why' question the new function validates the position.
6. The process of (5) should continue till you got a function which is not in the random list of functions. Hence, it is not a part of the project. That function will become the "lower order function" Which is also called "causative function" and also "assumed function".
7. At this point of time your critical path functions are identified.
8. Take one function from the critical path and try to identify from the random functions whether any function(s) happens at the same time or caused by the function on the critical path. Put that function under the function of the critical path and connect by vertical line. If there is more than one function, then put it in the descending order of importance.
9. Repeat (8) for all the functions on the critical path.
10. Identify if there is any 'one time function'. If it is there, then put that function beside the design objective. There may be more than one 'one time function' and may not there any.
11. The functions remaining will be the functions of "All The Time Function". But before putting it should be properly identified.

Technical FAST diagram: Based on the above procedure the FAST Diagram is drawn which is shown in Fig. 8.22.

8.3.5.3 Function-Cost Worksheet

The next will be to make a Function Cost Worksheet. This is shown in Fig. 8.23.

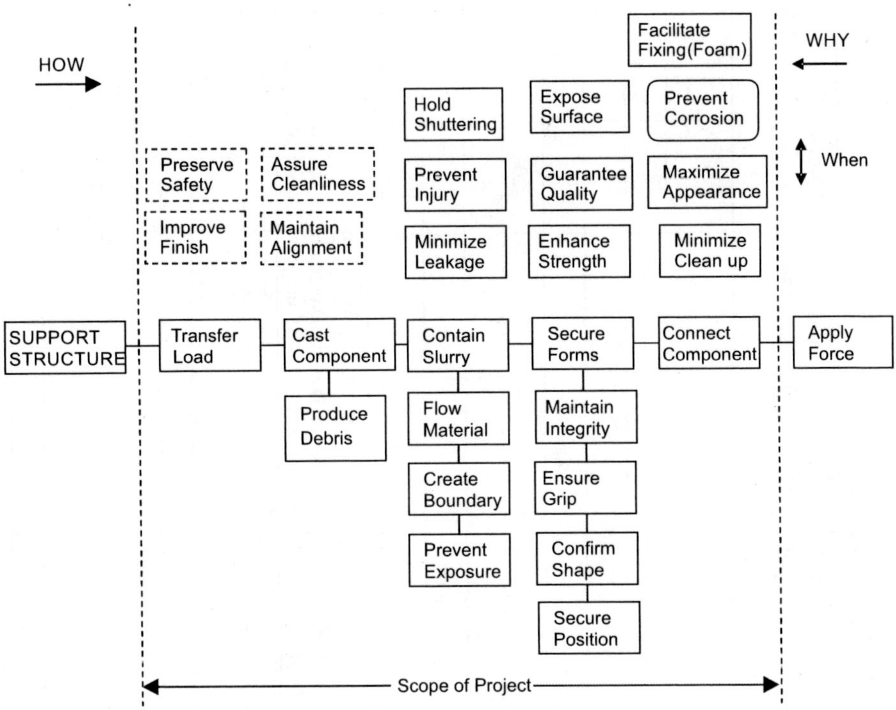

Fig. 8.22. Technical FAST Diagram.

8.3.5.4 Next Steps to Creativity Phase

The output of function phase is the input of creativity phase. The following are the outcomes from the Function Phase.

1. The functions on critical path of the Technically Oriented FAST.
2. The high cost functions in function-cost worksheet.
3. If the benchmarking is done for the same product, then mention the cost of those functions side by side of the functions of the project under review. The high gap function can be identified.
4. If benchmarking is not possible, then make the targets of high cost functions and put the target side by side.

The functions identified in the above four cases (some functions may appear in more than one place) are the potential functions. Ideas should be generated against each function to get the best alternative.

		All the time functions									
Activities	**Cost**	**Hold Shuttering**	**Prevent Injury**	**Minimize Leakage**	**Expose Surface**	**Guarantee Quality**	**Enhance Strength**	**Facilitate Fixing (Foam)**	**Maximize Appearance**	**Minimize Clean up**	**Prevent Corrosion**
Starter marking	487					487					
Reinforcement lapping	20,240						20,240				
Cover block fixing	27										27
Starter concreting	96	96									
Deshuttering	437				9			428			
Foam sheet fixing	165			145						20	
Shutter fixing	15		15								
Concrete pouring	1000						1000				
Slurry cleaning	16								16		

		Critical Path					Caused – By Functions							
Activities	**Cost**	**Transfer Load**	**Cast Component**	**Contain Slurry**	**Secure Forms**	**Connect Component**	**Produce Debris**	**Flow Materials**	**Create Boundaries**	**Prevent Exposure**	**Maintain Integrity**	**Ensure Grip**	**Confirm Shape**	**Secure Position**
Starter marking	6												3	3
Reinforcement lapping														
Cover block fixing	10									10				
Starter concreting														
Deshuttering														
Foam sheet fixing	145											145		
Shutter fixing	190				20	145					25			
Concrete pouring	3845	1696	1949	145				25	30					
Slurry cleaning	16						16							

Activities	Cost	Design Function			
		Preserve Safety	Assure Cleanliness	Improve Finish	Maintain Alignment
Starter marking	5318	5310			8
Reinforcement lapping	145		145		
Cover block fixing					
Starter concreting	9				9
Deshuttering					
Foam sheet fixing					
Shutter fixing					
Concrete pouring					
Slurry cleaning	14			14	

Fig. 8.23.

Case Study: 4

Value Engineering Study on "Sheet Galvanizing Process"

8.4 SHEET GALVANIZING PROCESS

8.4.1 Introduction

Hot dip galvanizing as a commercial process has been in vogue since the beginning of the last century and has evolved over the years to the present-day. The primary objective of galvanizing is to provide a protective coating of zinc on sheets. The coating has to be of adequate thickness so as to meet the demands of protection and customer preference with minimum dross and ash formation.

Zinc being a high value item, a small saving in its consumption has considerable effect on the overall cost of galvanizing. Consequently, the team undertook the subject to reduce zinc consumption in sheet galvanizing for this value engineering workshop.

8.4.2 Galvanizing Process

The major operations of any galvanizing process are:

1. Pickling and washing of the sheet.
2. Fluxing of the sheet.
3. Galvanizing the sheet.

The flow process chart is shown below:

Flow Process Chart

Processes Symbols

Pickle and wash sheet

To trough

Store

To galvanize pot

Flux

Galvanize sheet

To bed

Inspect sheet

Store galvanized sheet

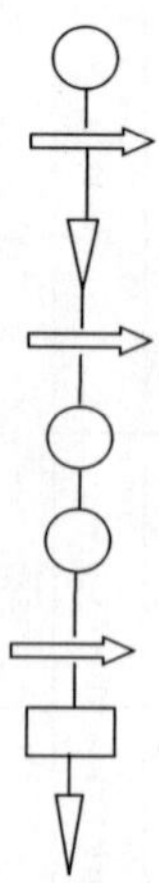

8.4.3 Function Analysis

The next step is to identify the functions in two words of all the activities in the process. This is shown in Table 8.14.

Table 8.14: Function Analysis of Galvanizing Process

Sr. No.	Activities of the Process	Items involved	Functions		Type
			Verb	Noun	
1	Pickle and wash sheet	Acid	Remove	Scale	B
		Water	Dilute	Acid	B
			Rinse	Sheet	S
			Remove	Iron-salt	S
		Steam	Produce	Heat	B
		Inhibitor	Prevent	Acid Attack	B
			Restrict	Acid-fumes	S
			Minimize	Iron-compounds	B
			Minimize	H_2 Absorption	S
		Wheat Bran	Restrict	Acid-fumes	S
2	To trough	Movement	Transport	Materials	B
3	Store	Placement	Store	Materials	B
4	To galvanize pot	Movement	Transport	Materials	B
5	Flux	Ammonium Chloride	Minimize	Iron-compounds	B
			Absorb	Moisture	B
			Prevent	Oxidation	S
		Tallow	Activate	Flux	B
6	Galvanize Sheet	Zinc	Deposit	Coating	B
			Enhance	Appearance	S
			Form	Dross	S
			Form	Flux-skimming	S
		Tin	Produce	Brightness	B
			Enhance	Appearance	S
		Antimony	Nucleate	Spangle	B
		Lead	Reduce	Drossing	B
			Protect	Pot	B
		Fuel	Produce	Heat	B
7	To bed	Movement	Transport	Materials	B
8	To inspect	Inspection	Qualify	Process	S
9	To store galvanize sheet	Placement	Store	Materials	B

The summary of functions are made and shown in Table 8.15.

Table 8.15: Summary of Functions

Basic Functions		Secondary Functions	
Verb	**Noun**	**Verb**	**Noun**
Remove	Scale	Rinse	Sheet
Dilute	Acid	Remove	Iron-salt
Produce	Heat	Restrict	Acid-fumes
Transport	Materials	Prevent	Oxidation
Store	Materials	Enhance	Appearance
Minimize	Iron-compounds	Form	Dross
Absorb	Moisture	Form	Flux-skimming
Activate	Flux	Qualify	Process
Deposit	Coating		
Produce	Brightness		
Nucleate	Spangle		
Reduce	Drossing		
Protect	Pot		

The function cost worksheet is shown in the Table 8.16.

Table 8.16: Function Cost Worksheet

Activity / Functions	Pickle and wash	Flux	Galvanize	Transportation	Store	Inspection	Total	%
Remove Scale	52						52.00	
Dilute Acid	0.03						0.03	
Rinse Sheet	0.01						0.01	
Remove Iron-salt	0.01						0.01	
Produce Heat	**88.00**		**112.00**				**200.00**	**8.1**
Prevent Acid Attack	0.25						0.25	
Minimize H_2 Absorption	0.25						0.25	
Restrict Acid-fumes	0.50						0.50	
Minimize Iron-compound	0.25	10.00					10.25	
Absorb Moisture		8.00					8.00	
Prevent Oxidation		4.00					4.00	
Activate Flux		0.05					0.05	
Deposit Coating			**1650.00**				**1650.00**	**66.9**
Enhance Appearance			**150.00**				**150.00**	**6.1**
Form Dross			100.00				100.00	
Form Flux-skimming			37.00				37.00	
Produce Brightness			30.00				30.00	

Enhance Appearance			12.00				12.00	
Nucleate Spangle			12.00				12.00	
Reduce Drossing			8.00				8.00	
Protect Pot			3.00				3.00	
Transport Materials				35.00			35.00	
Store Materials					50.00		50.00	
Qualify Process						100.00	100.00	
Total	**141.30**	**22.05**	**2114.00**	**35.00**	**50.00**	**100.00**	**2465.35**	**81.1**

8.4.4 Technically Oriented FAST

A Technically Oriented FAST is drawn based on the functions identified in Table 8.15. The final diagram is shown in Fig. 8.24.

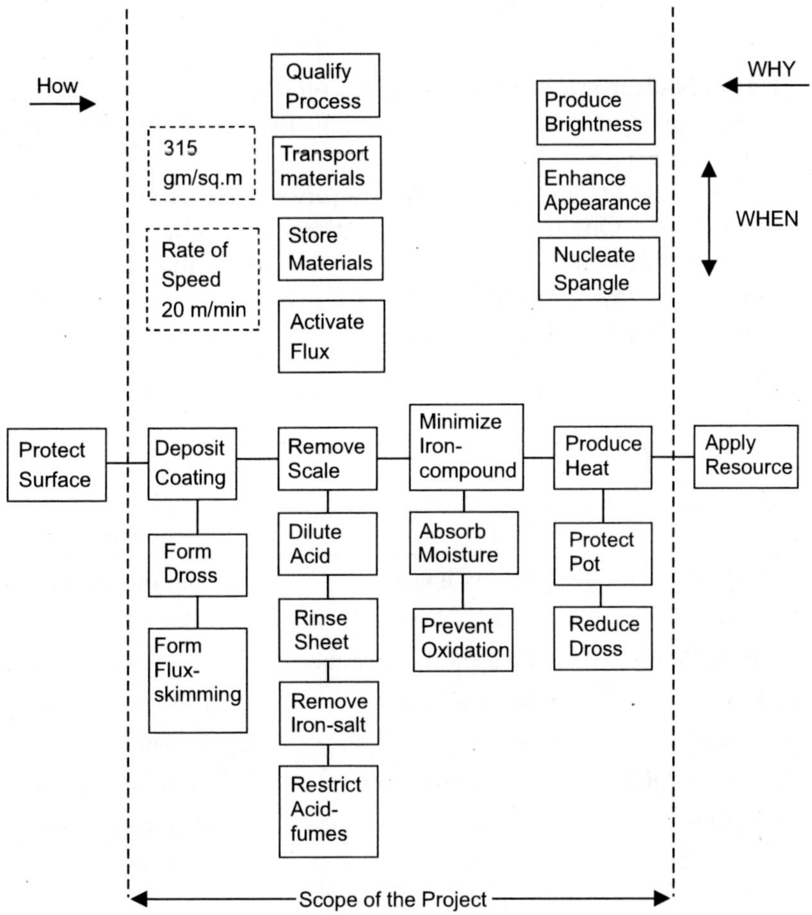

Fig. 8.24. Technically Oriented FAST.

Solutions

CHAPTER 1

1.

(a) This is clearly available in the chapter 1.
The product like "old stamp" has Esteem Value but does not have any Use Value.

(b) The activities in Software are equivalent to the components of Hardware. One has to define functions of each activity in Software, as one finds the functions of each feature of the components.

2. (b); **3.** (a); **4.** (c); **5.** (b); **6.** (d); **7.** (b); **8.** (c);
9. (a); **10.** (d); **11.** (c); **12.** (d); **13.** (c); **14.** (b)

CHAPTER 2

1.

Item	Work Function	Secondary Function
LCD Projector	Project Image	Improve Aesthetics
Fruit Juicer	Crush Object	Filter Object
Thermos Flask	Preserve Temperature	Facilitate Handling
Pulley	Reduce Effort	Reduce Friction
Road Median	Sedate Traffic	Enhance Safety
Hexagonal Bolt	Join Components	Withstand Torque
Paper Clip	Join Items	Prevent Corrosion
Adhesive Paper	Join Items	Indicate Manufacturer

2. To help the readers the work functions may be as below.

- Current: Motion object (Objects like water/air/electrons, etc.)
- Torque: Rotate object
- Volume: Measure quantity
- Energy conversion: Transform energy

3. (d); **4.** (c); **5.** (d); **6.** (a); **7.** (c); **8.** (a & c);
9. (b & d); **10.** (b); **11.** (c); **12.** (a); **13.** (d); **14.** (a); **15.** (b).

16.

Item	Work Function	Sell Function
Juicer	Crush Object	Filter Object
Grinding Machines	Maintain Tolerance	Assure Safety
Iron Box	Protect Object	Satisfy User
Flower Vase	Accommodate Objects	Improve Aesthetic
Door Hinge	Swing Object	Attract Customer
Pulley Drive	Transmit Torque	Assure Longevity
Toggle Switch	Make/Break Contact	Ease Operation
Decorative Paints	Reduce Corrosion	Create Distinction

CHAPTER 3

1. **Refer** Sec. 3.5;
2. Sec. 3.4
3. (d); **4.** (c); **5.** (a); **6.** (b); **7.** (d); **8.** (b);
9. (b); **10.** (a); **11.** (c); **12.** (a).
13. Refer to Sec. 3.4. The subsequent chapters will also help to answer this question.
14. (c); **15.** (d); **16.** (b)
17. Refer to Sec. 3.5

CHAPTER 4

1. Sec. 4.2 and Fig. 4.1
2. (c); **3.** (b); **4.** (d); **5.** (c); **6.** (b); **7.** (a);
8. (d); **9.** (c); **10.** (d) **11.** (a); **12.** (b); **13.** (d);
14. (c); **15.** (d); **16.** (c); **17.** (a); **18.** (b) **19.** (c);
20. (b).

CHAPTER 5

1.

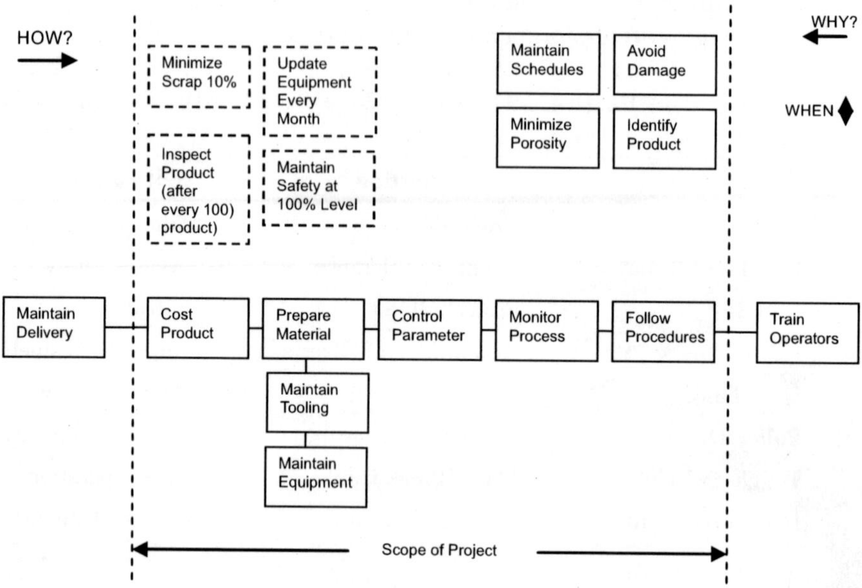

2. (c); **3.** (b); **4.** (a)

5.

Part	Feature	Functions	
		Verb	Noun
Bristle	Diameter	ensure	flexibility
	Rounded end	avoid	gum injury
	Bunch	support	cleaning agent
Body	Length (Top)	hold	bristles
	Length (Full)	ensure	reach
	Curvature	facilitate	handling
	Thickness & width	ensure	strength
	Under cut	facilitate	grip
	Under cut	reduce	weight
	Emboss	identify	manufacture
	Colour	attract	customer

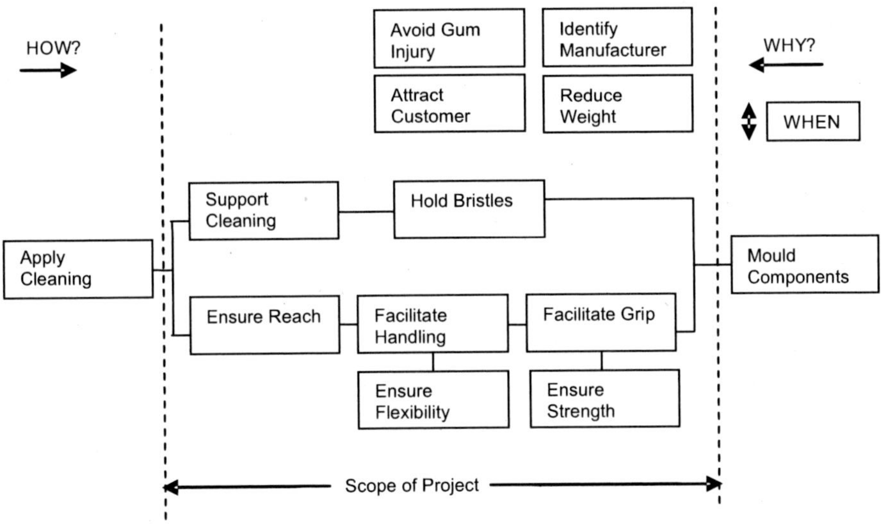

6.

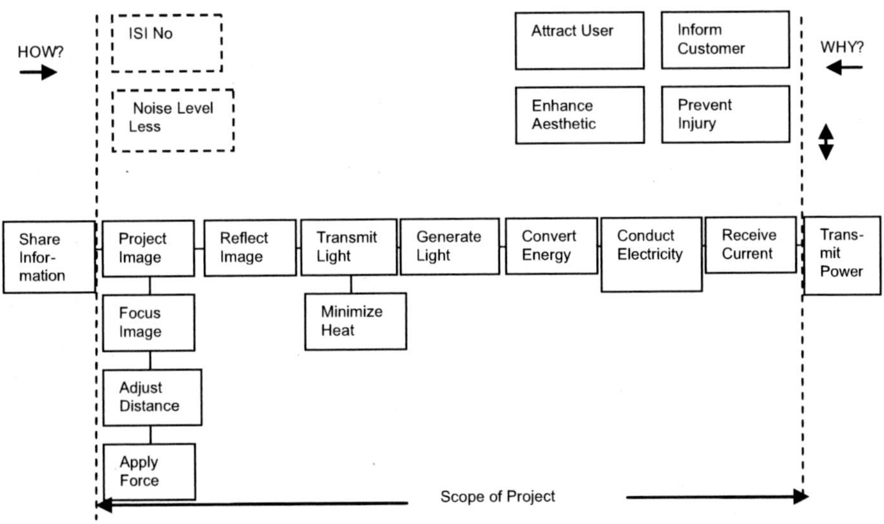

(*Source:* Functional Analysis Seminar for INVEST International VE Conference in Mumbai by Jim Bolton, PE, CVS, PVM)

7. Technically Oriented FAST

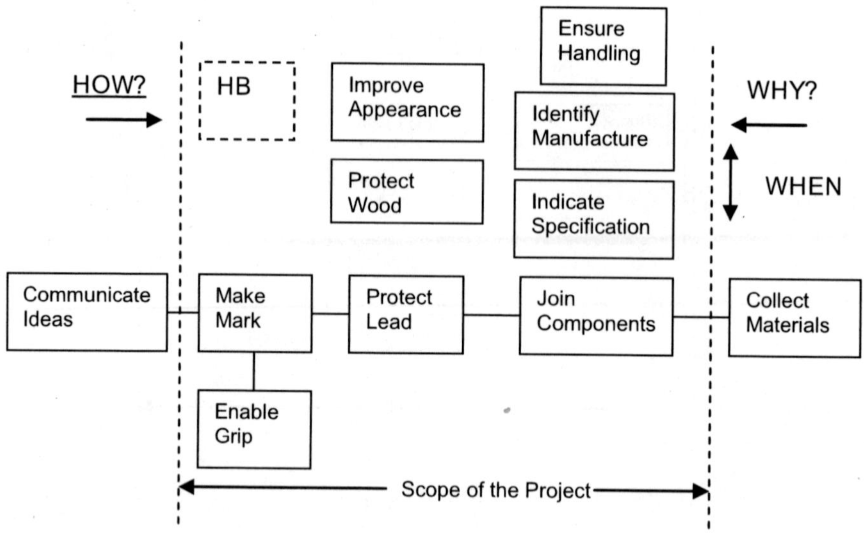

8. (b); **9.** (d); **10.** (b); **11.** (b); **12.** (d); **13.** (b);
14. Study Chapters 3 and 4 to have clear answer.
15. (c); **16.** (b); **17.** (d); **18.** (a); **19.** (b); **20.** (c);
21. (a) **22.** (b); **23.** (d)

CHAPTER 6

1. One can make comparative analysis of Technically Oriented FAST and Customer-Oriented FAST from the text itself.

2. Customer-Oriented FAST Diagram

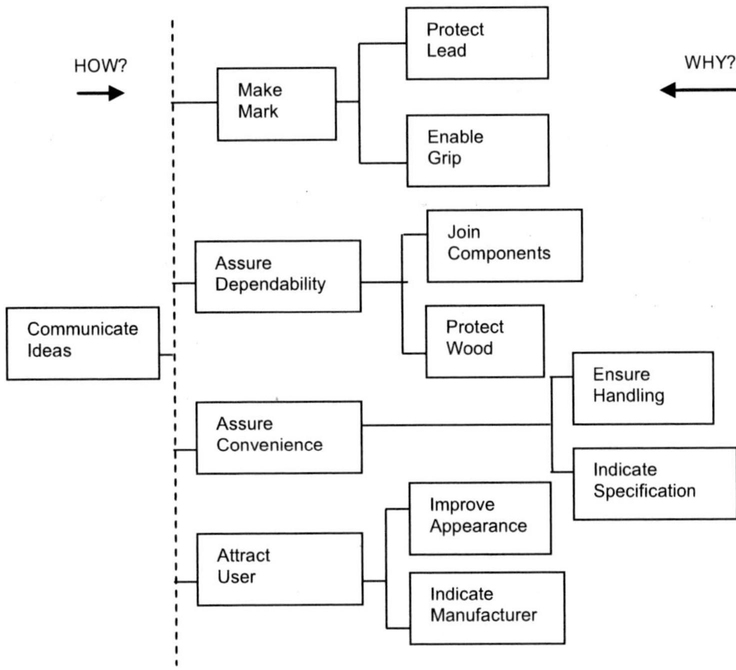

3. (c); **4.** (c); **5.** (b);

6. Read Sec. 6.4.6 to answer this question.

7. (b); **8.** (c); **9.** (d); **10.** (b); **11.** (c); **12.** (a);

13. (c); **14.** (b); **15.** (c); **16.** (b) **17.** (c); **18.** (a);

19. (a-D; b-C; c-B; d-A);

20. (a-D; b-A; c-B; d-C)

21. Read Chapters 3, 4 and 5 for proper answer.

CHAPTER 7

1. (c); **2.** (d); **3.** (a)

Glossary

In 1985, the Lawrence D. Miles Foundation founded the College of Fellows of the Society of American Value Engineers (SAVE), now SAVE International, with the specific intent of developing a Glossary of Terms related to value. Over a two-year period, approximately 10 Fellows worked individually and in teams to define, refine and finalize a glossary of value related terms. In 2006, the Glossary was reviewed by the Certification Board and those definitions most essential to the current application of value methodologies were identified and refined where necessary.

ASSOCIATE VALUE SPECIALIST (AVS): AVS is a recognition designed for individuals who are new to the value methodology. An AVS is encouraged to progress to VMP or CVS certification.

CERTIFIED VALUE SPECIALIST (CVS): CVS is the highest level of certification attainable through SAVE International. Designation is reserved for Value Specialists and Value Program Managers who have demonstrated expert level experience and knowledge in the practice of the value methodology.

COST: The expenditure of resources needed to produce a product, service, or process.

COST, LIFE CYCLE: The sum of all development acquisition, production or construction, operation, maintenance, use, and disposal costs for a product or project over a specified period of time.

COST MODEL: A financial representation such as a spreadsheet, chart, and/or diagram used to illustrate the total cost of families of systems, components, or parts within a total complex product, system, structure or facility.

FUNCTION: The original intent or purpose that a product, service or process is expected to perform. It is expressed in a two-word active verb/ measurable noun structure.

FUNCTION ANALYSIS SYSTEM TECHNIQUE (FAST): A graphical representation of the dependent relationships between functions within a project.

CLASSICAL FAST MODEL: A function displaying the interrelationship of functions to each other in a "how-why" logic. This was developed by Charles Bytheway.

HIERARCHY FUNCTION MODEL: A vertical "hierarchical" chart of functions. This places the basic function at the top. The function of each major system is placed beneath the basic function. The functions that support each of these functions are then placed on the next row. This process is continued until the team feels the level of detail is sufficient for the intent of the study.

TECHNICAL FAST MODEL: A variation to the Classical FAST that adds "all the time" functions, "one-time" functions and "same time " or "caused by" functions.

CUSTOMER-ORIENTED FAST MODEL: This variation of the FAST diagram was developed to better reflect that it is the customer that determines value in the function analysis process. Customer-oriented FAST adds the supporting functions: attract users, satisfy users, assure dependability, and assure convenience. The project functions that support these customer functions are determined by using the "how-why" logic.

FUNCTION ANALYSIS: The process of defining, classifying and evaluating functions.

FUNCTION, BASIC: The specific purpose(s) for which a product, facility, or service exists and conveys a sense of 'need'. In 'continuous innovation' projects the basic function must always exist, although methods or designs to achieve it may vary. In 'discontinuous innovation' projects, which seek to create new industries, the existence and persistence of the basic function is itself the focus of challenge.

FUNCTION COST: The expenditure of resources to perform the function.

FUNCTION, HIGHER ORDER: The specific goals (needs) for which the basic function(s) exists.

FUNCTION, LOWER ORDER (ASSUMED or CAUSATIVE): The function that is selected to initiate the project and is outside the scope of study.

FUNCTION, SECONDARY: A function that supports the basic function and results from the specific design approach to achieve the basic function.

FUNCTION, SELL: A function that provides a subjective expression of something that is to be achieved. In Function Analysis, sell functions are qualitative and are described using a passive verb and a non-measurable noun. Sell functions are also sometimes referred to as "aesthetic" functions.

FUNCTION, WORK: A function that provides an objective expression of something that is to be accomplished. In Function Analysis, work functions are quantitative and are described using an active verb and a measurable noun. Work functions are also sometimes referred to as "use" functions.

FUNCTION WORTH: The lowest overall cost to perform a function without regard to criteria or codes.

JOB PLAN: A sequential approach for conducting a value study, consisting of steps or phases used to manage the focus of a team's thinking so that they innovate collectively rather than as uncoordinated individuals.

PERFORMANCE: The capacity of a product to fulfill its intended function. Factors such as reliability, maintainability, quality and appearance are some examples.

PROJECT: A temporary endeavor undertaken to create a unique product, service, or result. For the purpose of Value Studies, a project is the subject of the study. It may be a physical product such as a manufactured item, or a structure, system, procedure, or an organization.

PROCESS: A sequence of activities that delivers a product or project.

SAVE INTERNATIONAL CERTIFIED PROFESSIONAL: For the purpose of a Value Study, the Job Plan shall be facilitated by a Certified Value Specialist (CVS), or a Value Methodology Practitioner (VMP) working under the supervision of a CVS. SAVE International Certification requirements are identified by the SAVE International Certification Board, which maintains a list of currently certified individuals.

SCOPE: The portion of the overall project that is selected for the value study. The analysis accepts everything within the defined scope in order to focus attention on the functions within those limits.

VALUE: An expression of the relationship between function and resources where function is measured by the performance requirements of the customer and resources are measured in materials, labor, price, time, etc. required to accomplish that function.

VALUE ANALYSIS: The application of value methodology to an existing project, produce or service to achieve value improvement.

VALUE ANALYST: See VALUE PROFESSIONAL.

VALUE ENGINEER: See VALUE PROFESSIONAL.

VALUE ENGINEERING: The application of a value methodology to a planned or conceptual project or service to achieve value improvement.

VALUE INDEX: A ratio that expresses function cost ÷ function worth. This ratio is used to determine the opportunity for value improvement, which is usually identified in the function analysis phase.

VALUE MANAGEMENT: The application of value methodology by an organization to achieve strategic value improvement.

VALUE METHODOLOGY: A systematic process used by a multidisciplinary team to improve the value of projects through the analysis of functions. (See Value Engineering, Value Analysis and Value Management).

VALUE METHODOLOGY ALTERNATIVE (or ALTERNATIVES): An alternative or alternatives prepared by the value study team and presented to management to provide financial and/or performance improvements and which is within the acceptable terms and conditions of the value study.

VALUE METHODOLOGY PRACTITIONER (VMP): VMP recognizes individuals with basic value training and some experience in the application of the methodology. Value methodology practitioners participate in or lead value studies.

VALUE PROFESSIONAL: One who applies the value methodology principles to study and search for value improvement. Synonymous with value analyst, value engineer, value practitioner, or value specialist.

VALUE PRACTIONER: See VALUE PROFESSIONAL.

VALUE STUDY: The application of a value methodology by SAVE International certified professionals using the Value Job Plan.

Source: Permission from SAVE International®, 136 South Keowee Street, Dayton, Ohio 45402 USA, www.value-eng.org

Bibliography

Bytheway, Charles W., (CVS), 1992 'FAST - An Intuitive Thinking Technique', SAVE Conference Proceedings, Phoenix, Arizona, June, pp. 229-232.

Fowler, Theodore C. (1983). 'The "User-Oriented" FAST Diagram', SAVE Conference Proceedings, Chicago, Vol. 18, pp. 89-94.

Fowler, Theodore C. (1993). [CVS, FSAVE], 'Function Analysis from Lawrence D. Miles By way of Charles W. Bytheway-A Chronology', INVAVE, (January-March): 17-23.

INVEST Website: - http://www.invest-in.org

Kannappan, L. (1992). [CVS (Life) EKS], 'Usage of Fast Diagrams Sharing Experience', INVEST Conference Proceedings, 10-11 November, Calcutta, pp. 16-28.

Kaufman, J.J. [CVS]. (1979). 'Function Analysis System Technique (FAST) for Management Application', SAVE Conference Proceedings, 23-26 May, Washington, DC, pp. 147-171.

Motion and Time Study Design and Management of Work by Ralph M. Barnes, John Wiley & Sons, Inc., pp. 63-65. Printed in USA.

Mukhopadhyaya, Anil Kumar, (2003). Value Engineering - Concepts, Techniques and Applications, Response Books, A Division of Sage Publication, 1st published.

Parker, Donald E. (1977). Value Engineering Theory, Washington DC: Lawrence D. Miles Value Foundation.

SAVE International website (Webpage link: http://www.value-eng.org/education_certificationprg.php):

Snodgrass, Thomas J. and Muthiah Kasi. (1986). Functional Analysis - The Stepping Stone to Good Value. Madison, WI: University of Wisconsin Press.

Tufty Harold, (1983). Compendium on Value Engineering; Bombay: The Indo-American Society.

Index